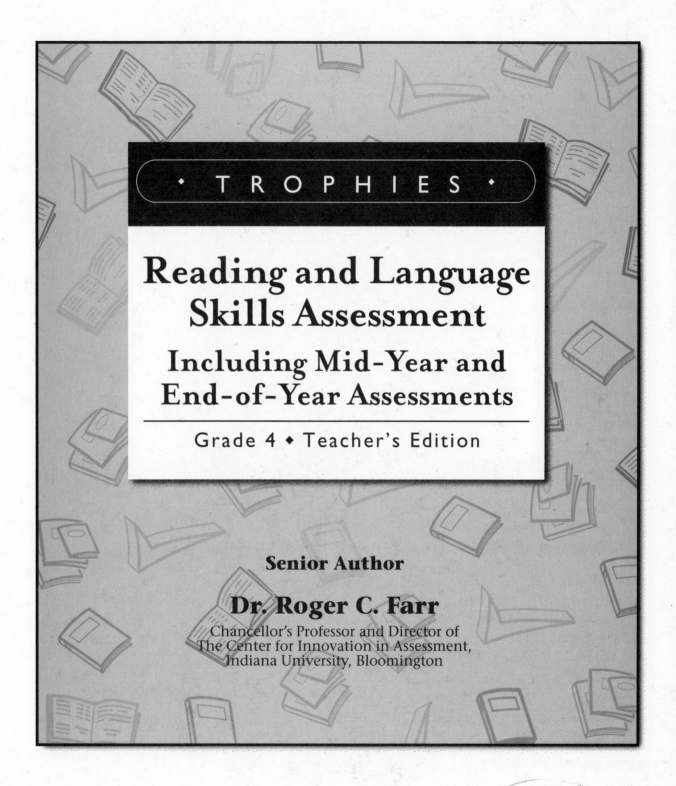

· TROPHIES ·

Reading and Language Skills Assessment

Including Mid-Year and End-of-Year Assessments

Grade 4 ◆ Teacher's Edition

Senior Author

Dr. Roger C. Farr

Chancellor's Professor and Director of
The Center for Innovation in Assessment,
Indiana University, Bloomington

**Harcourt**

Orlando   Boston   Dallas   Chicago   San Diego

Visit *The Learning Site!*
www.harcourtschool.com

Table of Contents

Appendix

Trophies
Assessment Components

• •

The chart below gives a brief overview of the assessment choices that are available at this grade level. The titles in boldface can be found in this Teacher's Edition.

Entry-Level Assessments	To plan instruction
Placement and Diagnostic Assessments	◆ To determine the best placement for a student and to diagnose strengths and weaknesses
Reading and Language Skills Pretests	◆ To determine a student's proficiency with selected skills *before* starting instruction
Formative Assessments	**To monitor student progress**
End-of-Selection Tests	◆ To monitor a student's comprehension of each selection
Oral Reading Fluency Assessment	◆ To monitor how automatically a student applies decoding skills
Assessment notes at "point of use" in the Teacher's Edition	◆ To monitor selected skills and strategies as they are taught
Mid-Year Reading and Language Skills Assessment	◆ To monitor how well a student has retained reading and language skills
Summative Assessments	**To assess mastery of skills taught** **To assess ability to apply skills and strategies**
Reading and Language Skills Posttests	◆ To assess mastery of reading and language skills taught in a theme
Holistic Assessment	◆ To evaluate a student's ability to apply reading and writing skills and strategies to new situations
End-of-Year Reading and Language Skills Assessment	◆ To evaluate mastery of reading and language skills taught during the year

Overview of the Teacher's Edition

●●

This Teacher's Edition is organized into two major sections. Each section contains information about a separate assessment component. The two assessment components are as follows:

Reading and Language Skills Assessments

Two parallel forms of the *Reading and Language Skills Assessments*, a Pretest and a Posttest, are available for each theme at this grade. These assessments evaluate the specific skills taught in the themes. The assessments can be used in tandem before and after instruction in the theme, or they can be used independently. For example, only the posttest could be used to evaluate how well students learned the skills taught in the theme.

Mid-Year and End-of-Year Skills Assessments

Two cumulative assessments are also included in this Teacher's Edition. The *Mid-Year Reading and Language Skills Assessment* evaluates the skills taught in the first half of the year in Themes 1 through 3. The *End-of-Year Reading and Language Skills Assessment* evaluates the skills taught during the entire year in Themes 1 through 6.

Copying masters for all of the assessment booklets are located in the Appendix. They are organized as follows:

Theme 1   *Reading and Language Skills Assessment*
Theme 2   *Reading and Language Skills Assessment*
Theme 3   *Reading and Language Skills Assessment*
Mid-Year Reading and Language Skills Assessment

Theme 4   *Reading and Language Skills Assessment*
Theme 5   *Reading and Language Skills Assessment*
Theme 6   *Reading and Language Skills Assessment*
End-of-Year Reading and Language Skills Assessment

Reading and Language Skills Assessments

Description of the Assessments

The *Reading and Language Skills Assessments* are criterion-referenced tests designed to measure students' achievement on the skills taught in each of the themes. Criterion-referenced scores help teachers make decisions regarding the type of additional instruction that students may need.

Six *Reading and Language Skills Assessments* are available at this grade level—one assessment for each theme. The assessments evaluate students' achievement in decoding, vocabulary, literary response and analysis, comprehension, research and information skills, and language. The formats used on the *Reading and Language Skills Assessments* follow the same style as those used in instruction. This ensures that the assessments are aligned with the instruction.

Scheduling the Assessments

The *Reading and Language Skills Assessments* have been designed to correlate with specific skills introduced and reinforced within each theme of the program. Therefore, a *Reading and Language Skills Assessment Pretest* could be administered before a theme is started to determine which skills need to be emphasized. Or, a *Reading and Language Skills Assessment Posttest* could be administered after a theme is completed to verify that students can apply the skills that were taught.

If possible, a *Reading and Language Skills Assessment* should be given in one session. The pace at which you administer the assessment will depend on your particular class and group. The assessments are not timed. Most students should be able to complete an assessment in thirty to forty-five minutes.

Directions for Administering

Accommodations can be made for students with special needs (e.g., special education, ELL). If accommodations are made for a student, they should be noted in the space provided on the cover of the assessment booklet.

Prior to administering a *Reading and Language Skills Assessment*, the following general directions should be read to the students.

Say: *Today you will be answering questions about some of the things we have learned together in class. Do your very best and try to answer each of the questions.*

When administering the assessment, repeat or clarify items that students do not hear or directions that they do not understand, but do not permit such explanations to reveal any answers.

The directions for each assessment are printed on the pages of the assessment booklets. There are no additional directions. If you wish, you may have students read the directions silently by themselves, or you may choose to read the directions aloud while students read them silently. Remember, if necessary, you may clarify any directions that students do not understand, as long as the clarification does not reveal any answers. Allow enough time for all students to complete the assessment or portion of the assessment being administered.

Scoring and Interpreting the Assessments

The *Reading and Language Skills Assessment* can be scored using the answer keys. Follow these steps:

1. Turn to the appropriate answer key in the Appendix.

2. Compare the student's responses, item by item, to the answer key and put a check mark next to each item that is correctly answered.

3. Count the number of correct responses for each skill or subtest and write this number on the "Pupil Score" line on the booklet cover. Add the Pupil Scores for each skill to obtain the Total Score.

4. Determine if the student met the criterion for each skill.

A student who scores at or above the criterion level for each subtest is considered competent in that skill area and is probably ready to move forward without additional practice. A column for writing comments about "Pupil Strength" has been provided on the cover of the assessment booklet.

A student who does not reach criterion level probably needs additional instruction and/or practice in that particular skill. Examine the student's scores for each subtest and decide whether you should reteach a particular skill, or move forward to the next theme.

For teachers who wish to keep a cumulative record of Pupil Scores across themes, a Student Record Form has been provided for that purpose in the Appendix.

A *Reading and Language Skills Assessment* is just one observation of a student's reading behavior. It should be combined with other evidence of a student's progress, such as the teacher's daily observations, student work samples, and individual reading conferences. The sum of all of this information, coupled with test scores, is more reliable and valid than any single piece of information.

Mid-Year and *End-of-Year*
Reading and Language Skills Assessments

Description of the Assessments

The *Mid-Year* and *End-of-Year Reading and Language Skills Assessments* are criterion-referenced tests designed to measure students' achievement on the skills taught in the themes. The assessments evaluate students' achievement in decoding, vocabulary, literary response and analysis, comprehension, research and information skills, and language. The assessments are designed to give a global picture of how well students apply the skills taught in the program. They are not intended to be diagnostic tests and do not yield specific scores for each skill. However, if a student does not reach the overall criterion for the total test, it is possible to judge his or her performance on the major skill categories (e.g., decoding, vocabulary, and comprehension).

The formats used on the *Mid-Year* and *End-of-Year Reading and Language Skills Assessments* follow the same style as those used in instruction. This ensures that the assessments are aligned with the instruction.

Contents of the Assessments

The following tables list the contents of the *Mid-Year* and *End-of-Year Assessments*. The contents of the *Mid-Year Reading and Language Skills Assessment* come from the skills taught in Themes 1, 2, and 3. The contents of the *End-of-Year Reading and Language Skills Assessment* come from the skills taught in Themes 1 through 6.

Mid-Year Reading and Language Skills Assessment

Skill Category	Subcategory	Objective	Items
Vocabulary	Prefixes, Suffixes, and Roots	Use prefixes, suffixes, and roots to determine or clarify word meaning	1–8
Literary Response and Analysis	Narrative Elements	Identify setting, characters, and plot in a story	9–11, 13
Literary Response and Analysis	Figurative Language	Identify and analyze figures of speech	12, 14
Comprehension	Text Structure: Cause and Effect	Analyze cause-and-effect relationships in text	20, 23–25, 28
Comprehension	Summarize	Recognize a summary of a passage	18, 30
Comprehension	Draw Conclusions	Use information from a reading selection and prior knowledge to form or support a conclusion	16–17, 19, 22, 27, 29
Comprehension	Text Structure: Compare and Contrast	Recognize and analyze text presented in a compare/contrast format	15, 21, 26
Language		Display command of standard English conventions	31–42

End-of-Year Reading and Language Skills Assessment

Skill Category	Subcategory	Objective	Items
Vocabulary	Prefixes, Suffixes, and Roots	Use prefixes, suffixes, and roots to determine or clarify word meaning	1–2
Vocabulary	Word Relationships	Use word relationships to determine word meanings	3–6
Comprehension	Text Structure: Cause and Effect	Analyze cause-and-effect relationships in text	12
Comprehension	Summarize	Recognize a summary of a passage	18
Comprehension	Text Structure: Main Idea and Details	Use text structure to identify the main idea and supporting details in a passage	10, 13, 16–17, 23, 25
Comprehension	Text Structure: Sequence	Recognize and analyze text that is presented in sequential or chronological order	11, 20
Comprehension	Follow Written Directions	Follow multi-step written directions	27–30
Comprehension	Author's Purpose	Recognize an author's purpose for writing	15, 21, 26
Comprehension	Elements of Nonfiction	Identify and use structural patterns in informational text to aid in comprehension	7, 22
Comprehension	Fact and Opinion	Distinguish between facts and opinions	8, 14, 24
Comprehension	Paraphrase	Recognize a paraphrase of a passage	9, 19
Research and Information Skills	Reference Sources	Use reference sources to locate information	31–34
Language		Display command of standard English conventions	35–50

Harcourt • Reading and Language Skills Assessment

Scheduling the Assessments

The *Mid-Year* and *End-of-Year Reading and Language Skills Assessments* have been designed to correlate with specific skills introduced and reinforced within each theme of the program. Each major reading skill taught in the program is represented on the assessments. The *Mid-Year* and *End-of-Year Reading Skills Assessments* are summative tests. That is, they are designed to evaluate whether students can apply the skills learned.

The *Mid-Year Reading and Language Skills Assessment* may be given after a student has completed the first three themes of instruction at this grade level. The *End-of-Year Reading and Language Skills Assessment* may be given after a student has completed the last three themes of instruction or the entire book.

The *Mid-Year* and *End-of-Year Reading and Language Skills Assessments* should be given in one session, if possible. The pace at which you administer the assessments will depend on your particular class and group. The assessments are not timed. Most students should be able to complete each assessment in approximately forty-five minutes to an hour.

Directions for Administering

Prior to administering the *Mid-Year* and *End-of-Year Reading and Language Skills Assessments*, the following general directions should be read to the students.

Say: *Today you will be answering questions about some of the things we have learned together in class. Do your very best and try to answer each of the questions.*

Distribute the assessment booklets and have students write their names on the Name line. Then have students fold the assessment booklet so that only the page they are working on is facing up. Make sure that every student understands what to do and how to mark the answers. When testing is completed, collect the assessment booklets.

The directions for each assessment are printed on the pages of the pupil booklets. There are no additional directions. If you wish, you may have students read the directions silently by themselves, or you may choose to read the directions aloud while students read them silently. If necessary, you may clarify any directions that students do not understand, as long as the clarification does not reveal any answers. Allow enough time for all students to complete the assessment.

Scoring and Interpreting the Assessments

The *Mid-Year* and *End-of-Year Reading Skills Assessments* can be scored by using the answer keys found in the Appendix. Follow these steps:

1. Turn to the appropriate answer key in the Appendix.

2. Compare the student's responses, item by item, to the answer key, and put a check mark next to each item that is correctly answered.

3. Count the number of correct responses for each skill category and write that number on the "Pupil Score" line on the cover of the assessment booklet. Add the Pupil Scores for each skill category to obtain the student's Total Score.

4. Next, determine if the student met the criterion for Total Score. The criterion score can be found on the cover page of the assessment booklet. Use the "Interpreting Performance" chart found in this section of the Teacher's Edition booklet to interpret the student's score.

5. If a student does not reach the overall criterion on the total test, you may evaluate the student's performance on particular skill categories. Look at each skill category and determine if the student met the criterion for that skill category. Then determine the student's strengths and weaknesses for particular skill categories. Write comments in the space provided.

There are 42 items on the *Mid-Year Reading and Language Skills Assessment* and 50 on the *End-of-Year Reading and Language Skills Assessment*. For each item, a correct answer should be given 1 point, and an incorrect or missing answer should be given 0 points. Thus, a perfect score on the mid-year assessment would be 42, and a perfect score on the end-of-year assessment would be 50. Use the following performance chart to interpret score ranges.

Interpreting Performance on the
Mid-Year and *End-of-Year Reading Skills Assessments*

Total Score	Interpretation	Teaching Suggestions
Mid-Year: 31–42 **End-of-Year: 37–50**	Average to excellent understanding and use of the major reading and language skills	Students scoring at the high end of this range exceed the criterion and should have no difficulty moving forward to the next level of the program. Students scoring at the low end of this range meet the criterion and are performing at an acceptable level.
Mid-Year: 0–30 **End-of-Year: 0–36**	Fair to limited understanding and use of the major reading and language skills	Students scoring at the high end of this range are performing slightly below the criterion and may need extra help before or after moving to the next level of the program. Note whether performance varied across the skill categories tested. Examine other samples of the students' work and/or administer some of the individual assessments (e.g., Phonics Inventory, Oral Reading Fluency Assessment) to confirm their progress and pinpoint instructional needs. Students scoring at the low end of this range do not meet criterion and should have their performance verified through other measures such as some of the individual assessments available in this program, or daily work samples. Identify what specific instructional needs must be met by reviewing the student's performance on each skill category.

A student who does not reach the criterion level may not do so for a variety of reasons. Use the questions that follow to better understand why a student may not have reached the criterion.

- *Has the student completed all parts of the program being tested on the assessment?*

If not, the results may not be valid, since the *Mid-Year Reading and Language Skills Assessment* evaluates all the major skills taught in the first three themes at this grade level, and the *End-of-Year Reading and Language Skills Assessment* evaluates all the major skills taught in Themes 1-6 at this grade level. It would be unfair to expect a student to demonstrate mastery of skills for which he or she has not received instruction.

- *Was the student having a bad day when he or she took the assessment?*

Students can experience social or emotional problems that may affect concentration and influence performance. Sometimes a problem at home or a conflict on the school playground carries over into the classroom and interferes with performance. Recall any unusual behavior you observed before or during the testing, or confer with the student to identify any factors that may have adversely affected performance. If the student's limited performance can be attributed to extraneous problems, readminister the assessment under better conditions or discard the results.

- *Does the student perform differently on group tests than on individual tests?*

Student performance can fluctuate depending on the context and mode of the assessment. Some students perform better in a one-on-one setting that fosters individual attention than they do in a group setting that is less personal. Others are more successful reading orally than reading silently. Likewise, some students feel more comfortable answering open-ended questions orally than they do answering multiple-choice questions on a paper-and-pencil test.

- *Does the student perform differently on tests than on daily activities?*

Compare the student's performance on the mid-year and the end-of-year assessment with his or her performance on other formal types of assessment, such as theme tests and standardized tests. Also note how the student's performance compares with his or her performance on informal types of assessment, such as portfolios, reading logs, and anecdotal observation records. If the results are similar, it would suggest that the mid-year and the end-of-year results are valid and accurately represent the student's performance. If the results are not consistent, explore alternative explanations.

To resolve conflicts regarding the student's performance, you may want to collect additional evidence. For example, you may want to administer some of the individual assessments available with this program (e.g., Phonics Inventory, Oral Reading Fluency Assessment).

As with all assessments, it is important not to place too much faith in a single test. The *Mid-Year* and *End-of-Year Reading and Language Skills Assessments* are just one observation of a student's reading behavior. They should be combined with other evidence of a student's progress, such as the teacher's daily observations, the student's work samples, and individual reading conferences. The sum of all this information, combined with test scores, is more reliable and valid than any single piece of information.

Appendix

• •

Answer Keys for *Reading and Language Skills Assessments: Pretests* and *Posttests*
Lead the Way/Theme 1

PRETEST	POSTTEST
VOCABULARY: **Prefixes, Suffixes, Roots**	**VOCABULARY:** **Prefixes, Suffixes, Roots**
1. B	1. D
2. A	2. B
3. D	3. A
4. A	4. C
5. C	5. B
6. B	6. C
7. C	7. A
8. B	8. B
LITERARY RESPONSE AND ANALYSIS: **Narrative Elements**	**LITERARY RESPONSE AND ANALYSIS:** **Narrative Elements**
9. B	9. C
10. C	10. D
11. B	11. B
12. D	12. B
LANGUAGE	**LANGUAGE**
13. C	13. B
14. B	14. D
15. D	15. C
16. A	16. A
17. B	17. C
18. D	18. B
19. B	19. B
20. C	20. C
21. A	21. A
22. C	22. C

Answer Keys for *Reading and Language Skills Assessments: Pretests* and *Posttests*
Lead the Way/Theme 2

PRETEST	POSTTEST
COMPREHENSION: **Text Structure: Cause and Effect** 1. B 2. C 3. A 4. D	**COMPREHENSION:** **Text Structure: Cause and Effect** 1. B 2. C 3. A 4. B
COMPREHENSION: **Summarize** 5. C 6. D 7. B 8. A	**COMPREHENSION:** **Summarize** 5. A 6. B 7. C 8. A
LITERARY RESPONSE AND ANALYSIS: **Figurative Language** 9. B 10. C 11. D 12. A	**LITERARY RESPONSE AND ANALYSIS:** **Figurative Language** 9. D 10. C 11. B 12. A
LANGUAGE 13. B 14. A 15. A 16. D 17. C 18. D 19. C 20. B 21. C 22. C	**LANGUAGE** 13. A 14. B 15. A 16. C 17. D 18. D 19. C 20. B 21. C 22. C

Answer Keys for *Reading and Language Skills Assessments:* *Pretests* and *Posttests*
Lead the Way/Theme 3

PRETEST	POSTTEST
COMPREHENSION: **Draw Conclusions**	**COMPREHENSION:** **Draw Conclusions**
1. A	1. B
2. D	2. C
3. C	3. B
4. A	4. A
COMPREHENSION: **Text Structure: Compare and Contrast**	**COMPREHENSION:** **Text Structure: Compare and Contrast**
5. A	5. B
6. C	6. D
7. D	7. A
8. B	8. C
9. C	9. C
10. D	10. A
11. B	11. D
12. B	12. B
LANGUAGE	**LANGUAGE**
13. A	13. D
14. B	14. C
15. D	15. B
16. A	16. D
17. C	17. C
18. B	18. A
19. D	19. B
20. C	20. D
21. A	21. A
22. B	22. C

Teacher's Edition

Answer Keys for *Reading and Language Skills Assessments:* *Pretests* and *Posttests*
Lead the Way/Theme 4

PRETEST	POSTTEST
COMPREHENSION: **Text Structure: Main Idea and Details**	**COMPREHENSION:** **Text Structure: Main Idea and Details**
1. B	1. B
2. D	2. A
3. B	3. C
4. A	4. A
COMPREHENSION: **Text Structure: Sequence**	**COMPREHENSION:** **Text Structure: Sequence**
5. B	5. B
6. D	6. C
7. A	7. D
8. D	8. B
COMPREHENSION: **Follow Written Directions**	**COMPREHENSION:** **Follow Written Directions**
9. B	9. A
10. D	10. B
11. C	11. B
12. A	12. D
LANGUAGE	**LANGUAGE**
13. A	13. A
14. D	14. D
15. B	15. B
16. A	16. C
17. C	17. C
18. A	18. A
19. D	19. C
20. B	20. B
21. B	21. A
22. C	22. B

Answer Keys for *Reading and Language Skills Assessments:* *Pretests* and *Posttests*
Lead the Way/Theme 5

PRETEST	POSTTEST
COMPREHENSION: **Author's Purpose**	**COMPREHENSION:** **Author's Purpose**
1. A	1. B
2. B	2. A
3. B	3. A
4. A	4. C
COMPREHENSION: **Elements of Nonfiction**	**COMPREHENSION:** **Elements of Nonfiction**
5. B	5. B
6. C	6. A
7. C	7. D
8. A	8. C
RESEARCH AND INFORMATION SKILLS: **Reference Sources**	**RESEARCH AND INFORMATION SKILLS:** **Reference Sources**
9. A	9. A
10. C	10. C
11. B	11. D
12. C	12. B
LANGUAGE	**LANGUAGE**
13. B	13. C
14. A	14. B
15. B	15. B
16. C	16. C
17. D	17. D
18. C	18. B
19. C	19. A
20. D	20. D
21. A	21. A
22. B	22. B

Answer Keys for *Reading and Language Skills Assessments: Pretests* and *Posttests*
Lead the Way/Theme 6

PRETEST	POSTTEST
VOCABULARY:	**VOCABULARY:**
Word Relationships	**Word Relationships**
1. C	1. B
2. B	2. D
3. C	3. C
4. A	4. A
COMPREHENSION:	**COMPREHENSION:**
Fact and Opinion	**Fact and Opinion**
5. D	5. C
6. B	6. D
7. C	7. B
8. D	8. A
COMPREHENSION:	**COMPREHENSION:**
Paraphrase	**Paraphrase**
9. B	9. B
10. A	10. C
11. C	11. A
12. A	12. B
LANGUAGE	**LANGUAGE**
13. D	13. B
14. A	14. C
15. B	15. B
16. D	16. A
17. A	17. C
18. C	18. D
19. A	19. A
20. B	20. B
21. A	21. A
22. D	22. C

Answer Key
Mid-Year Reading and Language Skills Assessment

VOCABULARY

1. B
2. C
3. D
4. C
5. B
6. D
7. A
8. B

LITERARY RESPONSE AND ANALYSIS

9. B
10. C
11. B
12. A
13. A
14. B

COMPREHENSION

15. D
16. C
17. A
18. B
19. B
20. A

21. D
22. A
23. B
24. C
25. D
26. C
27. B
28. A
29. B
30. C

LANGUAGE

31. C
32. B
33. A
34. D
35. B
36. B
37. C
38. B
39. C
40. D
41. C
42. A

Answer Key
End-of-Year Reading and Language Skills Assessment

VOCABULARY
1. B
2. C
3. A
4. D
5. C
6. B

COMPREHENSION
7. A
8. C
9. B
10. D
11. C
12. B
13. B
14. C
15. A
16. D
17. C
18. B
19. B
20. A
21. C
22. A
23. B
24. D
25. B
26. A
27. C
28. D
29. B
30. A

RESEARCH AND INFORMATION SKILLS
31. A
32. C
33. B
34. A

LANGUAGE
35. C
36. B
37. D
38. C
39. A
40. C
41. B
42. B
43. D
44. A
45. C
46. D
47. B
48. C
49. B
50. A

Student Record Form
Reading and Language Skills Assessment
Trophies
Grade 4

Name _____ Grade _____

Teacher _____

	CRITERION SCORE	PUPIL SCORE	COMMENTS
Theme 1			
Prefixes, suffixes, and roots	6/8	___/8	_____
Narrative elements	3/4	___/4	_____
Language	7/10	___/10	_____
Theme 2			
Text Structure: cause and effect	3/4	___/4	_____
Summarize	3/4	___/4	_____
Figurative language	3/4	___/4	_____
Language	7/10	___/10	_____
Theme 3			
Draw Conclusions	3/4	___/4	_____
Text Structure: compare and contrast	6/8	___/8	_____
Language	7/10	___/10	_____

Teacher's Edition

Student Record Form
Reading and Language Skills Assessment
Trophies
Grade 4

Name _____ Grade _____

Teacher _____

	CRITERION SCORE	PUPIL SCORE	COMMENTS
Theme 4			
Text Structure: Main idea and details	3/4	___/4	_____
Text structure: sequence	3/4	___/4	_____
Follow written directions	3/4	___/4	_____
Language	7/10	___/10	_____
Theme 5			
Author's purpose	3/4	___/4	_____
Elements of nonfiction	3/4	___/4	_____
Reference sources	3/4	___/4	_____
Language	7/10	___/10	_____
Theme 6			
Word relationships	3/4	___/4	_____
Fact and opinion	3/4	___/4	_____
Paraphrase	3/4	___/4	_____
Language	7/10	___/10	_____

· T R O P H I E S ·

Reading and Language Skills
Assessment Pretest

Lead the Way • Theme 1

Name _____ Date _____

SKILL AREA	Criterion Score	Pupil Score	Pupil Strength
VOCABULARY Prefixes, Suffixes, and Roots	6/8	_____	_____
LITERARY RESPONSE AND ANALYSIS Narrative Elements	3/4	_____	_____
LANGUAGE Sentences Declarative and Interrogative Sentences Imperative and Exclamatory Sentences Subjects and Predicates Complete and Simple Subjects	7/10	_____	_____
		_____	_____
TOTAL SCORE	16/22		

Were accommodations made in administering this test? ☐ Yes ☐ No

Type of accommodations: _____

_____

VOCABULARY: Prefixes, Suffixes, and Roots

Directions: Read each sentence. Fill in the answer circle in front of the correct answer for each question.

1. The frightened man's words were nonsense.

   What does the word *nonsense* mean?
   Ⓐ before sense
   Ⓑ not making sense
   Ⓒ above sense
   Ⓓ sense again

2. Which prefix can be added to the word *impose* to make it mean "impose above"?
   Ⓐ super
   Ⓑ pre
   Ⓒ non
   Ⓓ in

3. Which prefix can be added to the word *national* to make it mean "between nations"?
   Ⓐ mis
   Ⓑ re
   Ⓒ dis
   Ⓓ inter

4. The deer's alertness saved its life.

   What does the word *alertness* mean?
   Ⓐ state of being alert
   Ⓑ without being alert
   Ⓒ one who is alert
   Ⓓ resembling alert

GO ON ▶

VOCABULARY: Prefixes, Suffixes, and Roots (continued)

5. Suzy is the fastest runner in the class.

   What does the word *runner* mean?

   Ⓐ without running

   Ⓑ capable of running

   Ⓒ one who runs

   Ⓓ relating to running

6. Which suffix can be added to the word *music* to make it mean "relating to music"?

   Ⓐ er

   Ⓑ al

   Ⓒ less

   Ⓓ est

7. Which word has the same root word as *telephone* and *phonic*?

   Ⓐ tender

   Ⓑ phrase

   Ⓒ phonograph

   Ⓓ physical

8. Which word has the same root word as *telescope*?

   Ⓐ temperature

   Ⓑ telegraph

   Ⓒ scuttle

   Ⓓ scorpion

STOP

Harcourt • Reading and Language Skills Assessment

LITERARY RESPONSE AND ANALYSIS: Narrative Elements

Directions: Read the passage. Fill in the answer circle in front of the correct answer for each question.

Jimmy was feeling sad. When he got home from school, he called for his dog, Spike, to come play with him, just as he did every day after school. This time, though, Spike did not come.

"I think your dog may be gone," Mother said. "I saw him chasing a cat earlier today. I called for him to come back, but he kept on running after the cat. I haven't seen him since."

"What are we going to do?" Jimmy asked. "We've got to find him!"

"Don't worry," Mother said. "When it gets closer to supper time, I'm sure he'll find his way back home."

Jimmy went up to his room to do his homework, but he couldn't stop worrying about Spike. Later that evening, there was a scratching sound at the kitchen door. Jimmy ran to the door, opened it, and was relieved to see Spike there.

"Good boy! You're back! I missed you! Don't ever worry me like that again," Jimmy said.

9. The main character in this story is _____.
   Ⓐ a cat
   Ⓑ Jimmy
   Ⓒ Mother
   Ⓓ Spike

10. When does the story take place?
   Ⓐ before breakfast
   Ⓑ during school
   Ⓒ after school
   Ⓓ during the night

GO ON

Harcourt • Reading and Language Skills Assessment

LITERARY RESPONSE AND ANALYSIS: Narrative Elements (continued)

11. What is the problem in the story?

Ⓐ Mother will not let Jimmy have a dog.

Ⓑ Jimmy's dog is missing.

Ⓒ Jimmy's dog will not eat his food.

Ⓓ A cat owner is angry that Spike chased the cat.

12. How is the problem in the story solved?

Ⓐ Jimmy talks his mother into letting him get a new dog.

Ⓑ Jimmy builds a dog pen so that Spike can't chase the cat again.

Ⓒ Mother buys another kind of dog food for Jimmy's dog.

Ⓓ Jimmy's dog comes home, safe and sound.

STOP

Harcourt • Reading and Language Skills Assessment

LANGUAGE

Directions: Read each question. Fill in the answer circle in front of the correct answer for each question.

13. Which group of words is a **sentence**?

Ⓐ The peaceful waters.

Ⓑ Quickly ran down the steps.

Ⓒ She climbed the steep mountain.

Ⓓ Looked for a parking place.

14. Which group of words is a **sentence**?

Ⓐ Seemed excited and happy.

Ⓑ I couldn't wait to tell what happened.

Ⓒ A man with a long, gray beard.

Ⓓ The stampeding herd of cattle.

15. Which sentence has the correct **end punctuation**?

Ⓐ I can't find my missing sweater?

Ⓑ Grandma is eating her lunch now!

Ⓒ Is this your test paper.

Ⓓ Close the door when you go out.

16. Which sentence should end with a **period**?

Ⓐ Take an umbrella with you

Ⓑ When are we leaving on our trip

Ⓒ How lovely those flowers are

Ⓓ Did you close the window

GO ON

LANGUAGE (continued)

17. What **kind of sentence** is this?

    Will you help me with my lessons?
    Ⓐ declarative
    Ⓑ interrogative
    Ⓒ imperative
    Ⓓ exclamatory

18. What **kind of sentence** is this?

    Wow, I can't believe I won the contest!
    Ⓐ declarative
    Ⓑ interrogative
    Ⓒ imperative
    Ⓓ exclamatory

19. Which answer best describes the underlined word or words in this sentence?

    A white frost covered the grass like a blanket.
    Ⓐ simple subject
    Ⓑ complete subject
    Ⓒ predicate
    Ⓓ complete sentence

20. Which answer best describes the underlined word or words in this sentence?

    Many children entered the drawing contest.
    Ⓐ simple subject
    Ⓑ complete subject
    Ⓒ predicate
    Ⓓ complete sentence

LANGUAGE (continued)

21. Which answer best describes the underlined word or words in this sentence?

The <u>woman</u> baked some fresh bread.

Ⓐ simple subject

Ⓑ complete subject

Ⓒ predicate

Ⓓ complete sentence

22. Which answer best describes the underlined word or words in this sentence?

The woodsman <u>trimmed the branches</u>.

Ⓐ simple subject

Ⓑ complete subject

Ⓒ predicate

Ⓓ complete sentence

STOP

Harcourt • Reading and Language Skills Assessment

· T R O P H I E S ·

You Can Do It! / Theme 1
Reading and Language Skills Assessment

Harcourt

Orlando   Boston   Dallas   Chicago   San Diego

Part No. 9997-37747-8

ISBN 0-15-332203-9 (Package of 12)

4

TROPHIES

Reading and Language Skills Assessment Posttest

Lead the Way • Theme 1

Name _____ Date _____

SKILL AREA	Criterion Score	Pupil Score	Pupil Strength
VOCABULARY Prefixes, Suffixes, and Roots	6/8	_____	_____
LITERARY RESPONSE AND ANALYSIS Narrative Elements	3/4	_____	_____

LANGUAGE
Sentences
Declarative and Interrogative
   Sentences
Imperative and Exclamatory
   Sentences
Subjects and Predicates
Complete and Simple Subjects
	7/10	_____	_____

TOTAL SCORE	16/22	_____	_____

Were accommodations made in administering this test?　❑ Yes　❑ No

Type of accommodations: _____

_____

VOCABULARY: Prefixes, Suffixes, and Roots

Directions: Read each sentence. Fill in the answer circle in front of the correct answer for each question.

1. When I heard the news, I shook my head in disbelief.

   What does the word *disbelief* mean?
   - Ⓐ many beliefs
   - Ⓑ wrong belief
   - Ⓒ before belief
   - Ⓓ opposite of belief

2. Which prefix can be added to the word *summer* to make it mean "middle of summer"?
   - Ⓐ non
   - Ⓑ mid
   - Ⓒ pre
   - Ⓓ dis

3. Which prefix can be added to the word *write* to make it mean "write again"?
   - Ⓐ re
   - Ⓑ pre
   - Ⓒ super
   - Ⓓ under

4. It would be senseless to water the lawn when it is raining.

   What does the word *senseless* mean?
   - Ⓐ full of sense
   - Ⓑ capable of sense
   - Ⓒ without sense
   - Ⓓ one who senses

GO ON

VOCABULARY: Prefixes, Suffixes, and Roots (continued)

5. The lizard's color is changeable.

   What does the word *changeable* mean?
   Ⓐ without change
   Ⓑ able to change
   Ⓒ one who changes
   Ⓓ resembling change

6. Which suffix can be added to the word *dark* to make it mean "the condition or state of being dark"?
   Ⓐ est
   Ⓑ ful
   Ⓒ ness
   Ⓓ or

7. Which word has the same root word as *visual* and *vista*?
   Ⓐ vision
   Ⓑ villain
   Ⓒ vital
   Ⓓ voice

8. Which word has the same root word as *autograph*?
   Ⓐ attendant
   Ⓑ autobiography
   Ⓒ agriculture
   Ⓓ artificial

Harcourt • Reading and Language Skills Assessment

STOP

LITERARY RESPONSE AND ANALYSIS: Narrative Elements

Directions: Read the passage. Fill in the answer circle in front of the correct answer for each question.

Barbara's family flew from Texas to Germany. They arrived on a cold, rainy day in September. Barbara's father had just been assigned to a military base near Frankfurt. The family was not getting off to a very good start. They arrived late, and no place on the base was open for supper. They took a taxi to a restaurant near the base, but the menu was in German. Since they hadn't learned the language yet, they had to guess at what they ordered. When the waiter brought their food, Barbara ended up with liver soup! She ate a little of it, but she really didn't like liver at all.

"I'm not sure I'm going to like living here," Barbara said to her dad just before she went to bed that night. Everything is so different! I don't see how I'm ever going to learn to speak German."

"It'll get better, Barb," her father reassured her. "You're going to love traveling to France, Italy, and other countries. And starting tomorrow, you, Mom, and I will be taking German lessons. Once you learn a few words and phrases, you'll feel more at ease here. I bet you have already learned the words for liver soup!"

"You're right, Dad," Barb laughed. "I may be a fast learner after all!"

9. The main character in this story is _____.
- Ⓐ a restaurant waiter
- Ⓑ Dad
- Ⓒ Barbara
- Ⓓ Mom

GO ON

LITERARY RESPONSE AND ANALYSIS: Narrative Elements (continued)

10. Where does the story take place?
    Ⓐ Texas
    Ⓑ France
    Ⓒ Italy
    Ⓓ Germany

11. What is the problem in the story?
    Ⓐ Barbara does not want to fly to Germany.
    Ⓑ Barbara needs to learn a new language and adjust to a new country.
    Ⓒ Barbara's family cannot find housing near the military base.
    Ⓓ Barbara's father does not like his new job.

12. How is the problem in the story solved?
    Ⓐ Barbara overcomes a fear of flying.
    Ⓑ Barbara realizes she will feel better once she learns to speak German.
    Ⓒ Barbara's family finds a house in a small village near the base.
    Ⓓ Barbara's dad gets a different job back in the United States.

STOP

Harcourt • Reading and Language Skills Assessment

LANGUAGE

Directions: Read each question. Fill in the answer circle in front of the correct answer for each question.

13. Which group of words is a **sentence**?
    Ⓐ The peaceful waters.
    Ⓑ He packed his camping gear.
    Ⓒ Slowly moved down the path.
    Ⓓ Wished for a happy ending.

14. Which group of words is a **sentence**?
    Ⓐ Wanted new sneakers.
    Ⓑ The long, dusty trail.
    Ⓒ A large flock of geese in the sky.
    Ⓓ The camels drank water before the trip.

15. Which sentence has the correct **end punctuation**?
    Ⓐ I want to go to the museum?
    Ⓑ We wrote our names on the top line!
    Ⓒ Put on a heavy coat, please.
    Ⓓ What grade did you make.

16. Which sentence should end with an **exclamation point**?
    Ⓐ What a beautiful sunrise that is
    Ⓑ How much does the game cost
    Ⓒ Put a stamp on your letter
    Ⓓ May I borrow a pencil

GO ON

LANGUAGE (continued)

17. What **kind of sentence** is this?

Help me change the flat tire.

Ⓐ declarative

Ⓑ interrogative

Ⓒ imperative

Ⓓ exclamatory

18. What **kind of sentence** is this?

How many jelly beans are in the jar?

Ⓐ declarative

Ⓑ interrogative

Ⓒ imperative

Ⓓ exclamatory

19. Which answer best describes the underlined word or words in this sentence?

The cold weather is hurting the crops.

Ⓐ simple subject

Ⓑ complete subject

Ⓒ predicate

Ⓓ complete sentence

20. Which answer best describes the underlined word or words in this sentence?

Sara finished her science project.

Ⓐ simple subject

Ⓑ complete subject

Ⓒ predicate

Ⓓ complete sentence

GO ON

Harcourt • Reading and Language Skills Assessment

LANGUAGE (continued)

21. Which answer best describes the underlined word or words in this sentence?

    My wool <u>coat</u> kept me warm.
    Ⓐ simple subject
    Ⓑ complete subject
    Ⓒ predicate
    Ⓓ complete sentence

22. Which answer best describes the word or words in this sentence?

    The penguins <u>glided across the frozen pond</u>.
    Ⓐ simple subject
    Ⓑ complete subject
    Ⓒ predicate
    Ⓓ complete sentence

STOP

· TROPHIES ·

You Can Do It! / Theme 1
Reading and Language Skills Assessment

Harcourt

Orlando Boston Dallas Chicago San Diego

Part No. 9997-37741-9

ISBN 0-15-332203-9 (Package of 12)

4

TROPHIES

Reading and Language Skills Assessment Pretest

Lead the Way • Theme 2

Name _____ Date _____

SKILL AREA	Criterion Score	Pupil Score	Pupil Strength
COMPREHENSION			
Cause and Effect	3/4	_____	_____
Summarize	3/4	_____	_____
LITERARY RESPONSE AND ANALYSIS			
Figurative Language	3/4	_____	_____
LANGUAGE	7/10	_____	_____
Complete and Simple Predicates			
Compound Subjects and Predicates			
Simple and Compound Sentences			
Clauses			
Complex Sentences		_____	_____
TOTAL SCORE	16/22		

Were accommodations made in administering this test? ❑ Yes ❑ No

Type of accommodations: _____

_____

COMPREHENSION: Cause and Effect

Directions: Read the passage. Fill in the answer circle in front of the correct answer for each question.

Stella saw her new neighbor, Mrs. Reed, sitting on the front porch of her house. Mrs. Reed looked sad and lonely, so Stella walked over to see her.

"You seem a little unhappy, Mrs. Reed," Stella said. "Is there anything I can do to help?"

Mrs. Reed sighed and said, "I suppose I'm just lonely. I haven't met many people in this town yet. I miss my friends where I used to live. The days seem long when you don't have anyone to talk to."

Later Stella went home, but that night she had an idea. "Mom," Stella asked, "could we give one of Lady's puppies to Mrs. Reed? I think she would give the puppy a good home, and the puppy might cheer her up."

"That's a great idea, Stella," Mom answered.

The next day Stella took a small golden puppy to Mrs. Reed. She told her that the puppy was a gift to keep her company. Mrs. Reed's face broke into a wide grin. Then she said, "I never would have thought of getting a pet to keep me company, Stella. You figured out just what to do to make me happy."

1. In the beginning of the story, why does Stella walk over to see Mrs. Reed?
   Ⓐ Stella's mom tells her to go and welcome the new neighbor.
   Ⓑ Stella thinks that Mrs. Reed looked sad and lonely.
   Ⓒ Stella goes to get Lady out of Mrs. Reed's yard.
   Ⓓ Mrs. Reed invites Stella to come over to visit.

GO ON

COMPREHENSION: Cause and Effect (continued)

2. Why does Mrs. Reed think the days seem long?
   Ⓐ She has too much work to do.
   Ⓑ People in town keep bothering her.
   Ⓒ She has no friends to talk to.
   Ⓓ She misses a pet she has lost.

3. Why does Stella ask if she may give Mrs. Reed a puppy?
   Ⓐ She thinks the puppy will cheer up Mrs. Reed.
   Ⓑ She wants to keep Lady's puppies near her house.
   Ⓒ Her mom says she cannot keep all the puppies.
   Ⓓ Mrs. Reed asks her if she may have a puppy.

4. What effect does giving the puppy to Mrs. Reed have?
   Ⓐ Mrs. Reed gets upset that the puppy will cause damage.
   Ⓑ Mrs. Reed hopes that she can get some more puppies.
   Ⓒ Mrs. Reed worries about how to care for the pet.
   Ⓓ Mrs. Reed feels happier and less lonely.

COMPREHENSION: Summarize

Directions: Read each passage. Fill in the answer circle in front of the correct answer for each question.

The Garza family had many things to do today. The weekend of the family picnic had finally arrived, and it was to be held in their backyard.

Carlos had to trim the bushes and mow the yard so that his younger brother, Joe, could arrange the tables and set up the folding chairs. Dad was cleaning the large barbecue grill and before long would start the fire. Mom had been cooking since dawn, with Delores and Frankie as her assistants. Will, the youngest, spent his time licking cake batter from the mixing bowls.

The morning was warm, and Joe's muscles ached. He wondered whether a family gathering was worth all this effort. Then he remembered that his grandmother always said that no matter what happens in life, you will always have your family to fall back on. He smiled at the memory and went back to work.

5. Which statement is the best summary of this passage?
   Ⓐ Carlos trimmed bushes and mowed the lawn.
   Ⓑ Mom, Delores, and Frankie started cooking at dawn.
   Ⓒ The Garzas had many things to do to prepare for an important family event.
   Ⓓ Dad cleaned the barbecue grill for a family picnic.

6. Which is the most important idea to include in a summary of the last paragraph?
   Ⓐ Joe's muscles ached.
   Ⓑ Joe went back to work.
   Ⓒ It was a warm morning.
   Ⓓ Joe realized how important family is.

GO ON

COMPREHENSION: Summarize (continued)

> When people think of a cactus, they usually think of a thorny plant. Most cactus plants have hard, piercing thorns or tiny little spines that can get under a person's skin and hurt. Cactus plants, though, can provide food and water for both animals and humans. You just have to get past the thorns—and there are ways to do that.
>
> The prickly pear is one kind of cactus that is often used for food. It has both long thorns and small, irritating spines. Somehow over the years, people have developed a taste for the prickly pear. To prepare a prickly pear for eating, you must first scrape or burn the spines off— and it is not an easy job. For either job, you need heavy gloves and someone who knows how to do it. Fortunately for people who enjoy this food, a spineless type of the plant has been developed for people and livestock to eat. Usually called *Nopalitos*, prickly pears are sold in stores as far west as San Francisco and as far east as New York City.

7. Which is the best summary of the first paragraph of this passage?
    - (A) Most people think of thorns when they think of a cactus.
    - (B) Humans and animals can eat cactus plants once the thorns are removed.
    - (C) When the thorns or little spines of cactus get under a person's skin, they hurt.
    - (D) Most cactus plants have hard, piercing thorns.

8. Which is the most important idea to include in a summary of the second paragraph?
    - (A) A spineless type of prickly pear has been developed for people and animals to eat.
    - (B) The prickly pear has both long thorns and small spines.
    - (C) You need heavy gloves to scrape spines off prickly pears.
    - (D) Prickly pears are sold in stores in San Francisco and in New York City.

STOP

Score _____   *Lead the Way / Theme 2*

Harcourt • Reading and Language Skills Assessment

LITERARY RESPONSE AND ANALYSIS: Figurative Language

Directions: Read each passage or sentence. Fill in the answer circle in front of the correct answer for each question.

Lisa and her father walked on the sandy edge of the lake. The water was as calm as a sheet of glass. In the sky, the clouds were huge balls of cotton. The warm summer day made Lisa think how good the cool water would feel. She walked to the end of a wooden pier with her dad and dangled her feet in the lake. The water was very cold, but it was also very refreshing.

9. Which group of words in this passage is a metaphor?
   Ⓐ sandy edge of the lake
   Ⓑ were huge balls of cotton
   Ⓒ cool water
   Ⓓ also very refreshing

10. Read this sentence.

    The water was as calm as a sheet of glass.

    Why does the author compare the water to a sheet of glass?
    Ⓐ because glass is very hard
    Ⓑ because glass breaks easily
    Ⓒ because glass is smooth and shiny
    Ⓓ because glass has sharp edges

GO ON

LITERARY RESPONSE AND ANALYSIS: Figurative Language (continued)

11. What type of figurative language is used in this sentence?

The kite danced at the end of the string and seemed to laugh with joy.

Ⓐ metaphor

Ⓑ simile

Ⓒ hyperbole

Ⓓ personification

12. Read this sentence.

I don't care for him because he blows his own horn too much.

What does "blows his own horn too much" mean?

Ⓐ He brags about himself.

Ⓑ He doesn't like music.

Ⓒ He plays a horn.

Ⓓ He has thin lips.

STOP

Score _____   *Lead the Way / Theme 2*

Harcourt • Reading and Language Skills Assessment

LANGUAGE

> **Directions:** Read each sentence. Fill in the answer circle in front of the answer that best describes the underlined word or words in each sentence.

13. Three children <u>entered the spelling bee</u>.
- Ⓐ simple predicate
- Ⓑ complete predicate
- Ⓒ compound subject
- Ⓓ compound predicate

14. My parents <u>enjoyed</u> our school play.
- Ⓐ simple predicate
- Ⓑ complete predicate
- Ⓒ compound subject
- Ⓓ compound predicate

15. The ink <u>stained</u> my shirt.
- Ⓐ simple predicate
- Ⓑ complete predicate
- Ⓒ compound subject
- Ⓓ compound predicate

16. The cowboy <u>roped and saddled</u> the horse.
- Ⓐ complete subject
- Ⓑ compound subject
- Ⓒ complete predicate
- Ⓓ compound predicate

GO ON

LANGUAGE (continued)

17. The wasps and the bees in our yard bother me.

Ⓐ complete subject

Ⓑ complete predicate

Ⓒ compound subject

Ⓓ compound predicate

18. The hikers made and packed sandwiches for their lunch.

Ⓐ complete subject

Ⓑ compound subject

Ⓒ complete predicate

Ⓓ compound predicate

19. Since my homework is done, I may play outside.

Ⓐ simple sentence

Ⓑ compound sentence

Ⓒ dependent clause

Ⓓ independent clause

20. Luke has a new hamster, and he showed it to me.

Ⓐ simple sentence

Ⓑ compound sentence

Ⓒ complex sentence

Ⓓ dependent clause

Harcourt • Reading and Language Skills Assessment

LANGUAGE (continued)

21. Because it was raining, we canceled our picnic.
- (A) simple sentence
- (B) compound sentence
- (C) dependent clause
- (D) independent clause

22. Since you are always careful, you may borrow my bike.
- (A) simple sentence
- (B) compound sentence
- (C) complex sentence
- (D) dependent clause

STOP

· T R O P H I E S ·

Side by Side / Theme 2
Reading and Language Skills Assessment

Harcourt

Orlando   Boston   Dallas   Chicago   San Diego

Part No. 9997-37748-6

ISBN 0-15-332203-9 (Package of 12)

4

TROPHIES

Reading and Language Skills Assessment Posttest

Lead the Way • Theme 2

Name _____ Date _____

SKILL AREA	Criterion Score	Pupil Score	Pupil Strength
COMPREHENSION			
Cause and Effect	3/4	_____	_____
Summarize	3/4	_____	_____
LITERARY RESPONSE AND ANALYSIS			
Figurative Language	3/4	_____	_____
LANGUAGE	7/10	_____	_____
Complete and Simple Predicates			
Compound Subjects and Predicates			
Simple and Compound Sentences			
Clauses			
Complex Sentences			
TOTAL SCORE	16/22	_____	_____

Were accommodations made in administering this test?   ☐ Yes   ☐ No

Type of accommodations: _____

_____

ISBN 0-15-332203-9

10   170   10 09 08 07 06 05

COMPREHENSION: Cause and Effect

Directions: Read the passage. Fill in the answer circle in front of the correct answer for each question.

Jim couldn't get to sleep. His mom and dad couldn't get to sleep either. Jim's new puppy, Max, kept whining and crying. Max was keeping the whole family awake. Jim went to the kitchen where Max was staying. He gave the pup water and food. Then he talked softly to make Max feel safe and loved. Still Max cried. He wouldn't go to sleep.

Dad said, "I think I know how to get Max to sleep."

First, Dad got a heating pad. He put it in the box where Max was supposed to sleep. He turned the heating pad on low, and felt it to make sure it wasn't too hot. Next, he put a clock beside the box. Very soon, Max was sleeping soundly.

"Why did a heating pad and a clock help Max go to sleep?" Jim asked later.

"Max missed his mother," Dad explained. "The heating pad feels warm like his mother's body. The ticking clock sounds like the beating of her heart. Now he feels cozy and warm."

1. In the beginning of the story, why can't Jim, Mom, and Dad get to sleep?
   Ⓐ They went to bed too early.
   Ⓑ Max is whining in the kitchen.
   Ⓒ They are excited about having a new pet.
   Ⓓ Max's mother is making noise outside.

2. Why does Dad put a clock beside Max's box?
   Ⓐ to give him something to play with
   Ⓑ to set the time to give him some food
   Ⓒ to sound like his mother's heartbeats
   Ⓓ to give him something to chew on

GO ON

COMPREHENSION: Cause and Effect (continued)

3. What does Dad say is making Max cry?

Ⓐ Max misses his mother.

Ⓑ Max wants to go outside.

Ⓒ Max is hungry.

Ⓓ Max is thirsty.

4. What effect does putting a heating pad in Max's box have?

Ⓐ Max is afraid of the heating pad.

Ⓑ Max feels warm and goes to sleep.

Ⓒ Max gets tangled in the cord.

Ⓓ Max starts to play with the heating pad.

STOP

Harcourt • Reading and Language Skills Assessment

COMPREHENSION: Summarize

Directions: Read each passage. Fill in the answer circle in front of the correct answer for each question.

Miranda's family was enjoying one last summer outing before school started—a day of hiking in the nearby mountains. As Miranda followed her family down the last leg of the trail, she slipped on a loose rock and fell with her left arm beneath her. She knew her wrist was hurt but didn't realize it was broken until her mother screamed. When they reached their car, they made a beeline for the closest hospital.

Before Miranda knew it, her arm was covered in an ugly cast. She was unhappy about starting fifth grade wearing a cast, but she decided to make the cast prettier by drawing colorful designs on it and by letting her family and friends write on it. "Now that's better," Miranda thought. "My cast has almost every color of the rainbow!"

5. Which statement is the best summary of the first paragraph of this passage?

Ⓐ During a day of hiking with her family, Miranda slipped and broke her wrist.

Ⓑ Miranda followed her family down the last leg of a hiking trail.

Ⓒ Miranda didn't realize her wrist was broken until her mother screamed.

Ⓓ Miranda and her family had planned one last summer outing in the nearby mountains before school started.

GO ON

COMPREHENSION: Summarize (continued)

6. Which sentence is most important to include in a summary of the last paragraph?

Ⓐ Miranda's cast had almost every color of the rainbow on it.

Ⓑ Miranda made the best of wearing an arm cast by letting her family and friends write on it.

Ⓒ Miranda's arm was covered in an ugly cast.

Ⓓ Miranda was unhappy about starting fifth grade.

COMPREHENSION: Summarize (continued)

Tracking dogs are specially trained to help find lost people. These dogs may be asked to find a lost child, a camper lost in the woods, or even someone injured in a small-plane crash. The dogs, according to their handlers, love their work and are eager to help.

For humans, seeing is believing. For dogs, though, smelling, or *scenting*, is believing. One of the first things a dog handler must learn is to trust the dog's nose instead of the handler's eyes. Dogs are trained very carefully to do this work. They learn to follow one scent among hundreds of others. They learn not to be confused by a "false" scent put in their path by their trainer. Trainers try many things to "trick" the dogs while training them. They might spray a trail with skunk spray or with a solution of alcohol, or they might put bowls of food in a dog's path. After many months of training, these tricks will not cause a good dog to lose the trail. Once the dog has sniffed something that has been worn or handled by the person the trainers are trying to find, the dog will follow that scent, no matter what. These brave and hardworking animals have saved many hundreds of lives.

7. Which statement is the best summary of the first paragraph of this passage?
   Ⓐ Tracking dogs may be asked to find a camper lost in the woods.
   Ⓑ Tracking dogs love their work and are eager to help.
   Ⓒ Tracking dogs are specially trained to help find lost people.
   Ⓓ Tracking dogs may be asked to find someone injured in a small-plane crash.

GO ON

COMPREHENSION: Summarize (continued)

8. Which is the most important idea to include in a summary of the last paragraph?

Ⓐ Tracking dogs must follow one scent and must not be confused by a false scent put in their path.

Ⓑ Trainers might spray a trail with skunk spray or with a solution of alcohol.

Ⓒ Trainers might put bowls of food in a dog's path.

Ⓓ For humans, seeing is believing.

STOP

Harcourt • Reading and Language Skills Assessment

LITERARY RESPONSE AND ANALYSIS: Figurative Language

Directions: Read each passage or sentence. Fill in the answer circle in front of the correct answer for each question.

Sarah stepped into the batter's box. The baseball game was tied, and she was very nervous. Her hands felt like bricks, and her legs were shaking. The pitcher threw the ball, and Sarah swung. It was a hit! Sarah ran to first base. In the stands, the crowd was a sea of cheering faces.

9. Which group of words in this story is a metaphor?
Ⓐ baseball game was tied
Ⓑ legs were shaking
Ⓒ ran to first base
Ⓓ was a sea of cheering faces

10. Read this sentence.

Her hands felt like bricks, and her legs were shaking.

Why does the author compare Sarah's hands to bricks?
Ⓐ because bricks are used to make buildings
Ⓑ because bricks are rough and bumpy
Ⓒ because bricks are heavy and difficult to lift
Ⓓ because bricks are sturdy and thick

11. What type of figurative language is used in this sentence?

Our school bus is as yellow as a lemon.
Ⓐ metaphor
Ⓑ simile
Ⓒ hyperbole
Ⓓ personification

GO ON

LITERARY RESPONSE AND ANALYSIS: Figurative Language (continued)

12. Read this sentence.

I made a beeline for the nearest exit.

What does "made a beeline" mean?
(A) went quickly by the shortest way
(B) dripped a trail of honey for some bees
(C) chased a swarm of bees
(D) drew a line

STOP

Harcourt • Reading and Language Skills Assessment

LANGUAGE

Directions: Read each sentence. Fill in the answer circle in front of the answer that best describes the underlined word or words in each sentence.

13. My older brother <u>reads</u> the newspaper.
   Ⓐ simple predicate
   Ⓑ complete predicate
   Ⓒ compound subject
   Ⓓ compound predicate

14. The happy children <u>joined the game</u>.
   Ⓐ simple predicate
   Ⓑ complete predicate
   Ⓒ compound subject
   Ⓓ compound predicate

15. They <u>floated</u> across the pond.
   Ⓐ simple predicate
   Ⓑ complete predicate
   Ⓒ compound subject
   Ⓓ compound predicate

16. <u>Mike and Melanie</u> in my class are twins.
   Ⓐ complete subject
   Ⓑ complete predicate
   Ⓒ compound subject
   Ⓓ compound predicate

17. The woman <u>baked and served</u> fresh, hot bread.
   Ⓐ complete subject
   Ⓑ compound subject
   Ⓒ complete predicate
   Ⓓ compound predicate

GO ON

LANGUAGE (continued)

18. Dad <u>raked and bagged</u> the leaves.
    Ⓐ complete subject
    Ⓑ compound subject
    Ⓒ complete predicate
    Ⓓ compound predicate

19. <u>Because it was very cold</u>, Keith put on a hat.
    Ⓐ simple sentence
    Ⓑ compound sentence
    Ⓒ dependent clause
    Ⓓ independent clause

20. <u>Ellen slammed the door, and the baby woke up</u>.
    Ⓐ simple sentence
    Ⓑ compound sentence
    Ⓒ complex sentence
    Ⓓ dependent clause

21. <u>Since John arrived late</u>, we started dinner without him.
    Ⓐ simple sentence
    Ⓑ compound sentence
    Ⓒ dependent clause
    Ⓓ independent clause

22. <u>Because the ice is thin, you should not skate on the lake</u>.
    Ⓐ simple sentence
    Ⓑ compound sentence
    Ⓒ complex sentence
    Ⓓ dependent clause

Score _____

Harcourt • Reading and Language Skills Assessment

· T R O P H I E S ·

Side by Side / Theme 2

Reading and Language Skills Assessment

Orlando   Boston   Dallas   Chicago   San Diego

Part No. 9997-37742-7

ISBN 0-15-332203-9 (Package of 12)

4

TROPHIES

Reading and Language Skills
Assessment Pretest

Lead the Way • Theme 3

Name _____ Date _____

SKILL AREA	Criterion Score	Pupil Score	Pupil Strength
COMPREHENSION			
Draw Conclusions	3/4	_____	_____
Compare and Contrast	6/8	_____	_____
LANGUAGE	7/10	_____	_____
Common and Proper Nouns			
Singular and Plural Nouns			
Possessive Nouns			
Abbreviations			
Pronouns and Antecedents			
TOTAL SCORE	16/22	_____	_____

Were accommodations made in administering this test? ☐ Yes ☐ No

Type of accommodations: _____

_____

COMPREHENSION: Draw Conclusions

Directions: Read the passage. Fill in the answer circle in front of the correct answer for each question.

I found a raccoon last spring during a camping trip. I took it home and fed it warm milk through a straw. Now it weighs more than fifteen pounds, and it eats everything. Mr. Brown, our neighbor, has said, "Bob, if your raccoon gets into my garden one more time, I'll make a coonskin cap out of him!" Eating isn't the only problem. My sister was really upset when my raccoon hid her gold ring in its nest.

It is spring again, and my raccoon seems restless. We ride slowly up the river in my canoe. We hear the sound of another raccoon on the shore. My raccoon answers with a soft call. Suddenly, it dives into the water and swims toward the sound. I wait for a long, long time. Finally, I turn the canoe around and paddle slowly home.

1. The raccoon that Bob found was probably from _____.
   Ⓐ the wild
   Ⓑ a pet shop
   Ⓒ the circus
   Ⓓ a zoo

2. What word would Mr. Brown and Bob's sister use to describe the raccoon?
   Ⓐ adorable
   Ⓑ playful
   Ⓒ silly
   Ⓓ bothersome

GO ON

COMPREHENSION: Draw Conclusions (continued)

3. Bob's raccoon jumped out of the boat because it wanted to _____.

   Ⓐ drink some water

   Ⓑ swim to Bob's house

   Ⓒ join the other raccoon

   Ⓓ play a game with Bob

4. At the end of the story, Bob most likely felt _____.

   Ⓐ sad

   Ⓑ angry

   Ⓒ shy

   Ⓓ happy

Harcourt • Reading and Language Skills Assessment

COMPREHENSION: Compare and Contrast

Directions: Read each passage. Fill in the answer circle in front of the correct answer for each question.

Lions and tigers are the largest animals in the cat family. Some people say the tiger is fiercer than the lion, but the lion is still thought to be among the strongest and fiercest of all wild creatures.

The bodies of tigers and lions are similar, but they can look quite different. A lion's coat can vary from buff yellow, orange-brown, or silver gray to dark brown. Male lions usually have a mane, which may be short or long and light or dark. Tigers are known for their striped markings. Depending on the type of tiger and the place where it lives, a tiger's coat may be bright reddish-tan with dark stripes, or it may be paler or black and white. The tiger has no mane.

Both lions and tigers are meat eaters, and they usually hunt at night. They prefer to prey upon medium- to large-size animals such as zebras and antelopes, but they have been known to attack much larger animals.

Lions are unique among cats in that they live and hunt in a group, or *pride*. A pride is made up of several generations of lionesses (female lions), their cubs, and one or two adult male lions. Tigers usually live alone.

5. According to this passage, **both** tigers and lions can be described as _____.

- Ⓐ fierce
- Ⓑ quiet
- Ⓒ tame
- Ⓓ friendly

GO ON

COMPREHENSION: Compare and Contrast (continued)

6. One way tigers and lions are the **same** is that they both _____.
   - (A) have bright reddish-tan fur
   - (B) have manes
   - (C) are members of the cat family
   - (D) live in prides

7. The coat of a tiger is **different** from the coat of a lion because the tiger's coat has _____.
   - (A) spots
   - (B) thicker fur
   - (C) longer fur
   - (D) striped markings

8. One way tigers are **different** from lions is that tigers usually _____.
   - (A) hunt at night
   - (B) live alone
   - (C) eat meat
   - (D) attack antelopes

COMPREHENSION: Compare and Contrast (continued)

Carl and Rob asked Dad to take them swimming, and Dad said he would.

"I want to go to the city pool," Carl said. "I like to dive off the high diving board. There are always some kids from school there, too. It's fun to have other kids to have diving contests or swimming races with. We can eat banana snow cones from the snack bar after we swim."

"I don't like the city pool," Rob chimed in. "It's too crowded and noisy. Every time I try to swim the length of the pool, people get in my way. I don't like snow cones as much as you do, either. I want to go to Bayside Beach. We can have privacy there. We can go to a quiet part of the beach. Dad can rest on the sand while we swim. I like to build sandcastles, and we can do that, too. We can lie on the sand and read. We can even watch for gulls."

"The beach is too far away, and I don't like all the sand. It gets all over the food," Carl complained.

"Well, I don't want to go to the city pool," Rob said. "I like peace and quiet."

9. How are Carl and Rob **alike**?
   Ⓐ They both like the beach.
   Ⓑ They both like privacy.
   Ⓒ They both like to swim.
   Ⓓ They both like the city pool.

10. One way Carl is **different** from Rob is that Carl likes to _____.
   Ⓐ build sandcastles
   Ⓑ watch for gulls
   Ⓒ read on the beach
   Ⓓ dive from the high board

GO ON

COMPREHENSION: Compare and Contrast (continued)

11. One way Rob is **different** from Carl is that Rob likes to _____.

Ⓐ have diving contests

Ⓑ read on the beach

Ⓒ eat snow cones

Ⓓ swim races with other kids

12. Which word best describes **both** Carl and Rob?

Ⓐ helpful

Ⓑ determined

Ⓒ patient

Ⓓ nosy

STOP

Harcourt • Reading and Language Skills Assessment

LANGUAGE

Directions: Read each sentence. Fill in the answer circle in front of the correct answer for each question.

13. Which word is a common noun in this sentence?

    The jar could not be opened easily.
    Ⓐ jar
    Ⓑ could
    Ⓒ opened
    Ⓓ easily

14. Which word is a proper noun in this sentence?

    The mayor of Philadelphia gave a speech at our school.
    Ⓐ mayor
    Ⓑ Philadelphia
    Ⓒ speech
    Ⓓ school

15. Which word belongs in the blank to complete this sentence?

    We had cake, ice cream, and some fresh _____ for dessert.
    Ⓐ berry
    Ⓑ berrys
    Ⓒ berryes
    Ⓓ berries

GO ON

LANGUAGE (continued)

16. Which word belongs in the blank to complete this sentence?

    All the _____ on the trees have begun to change colors for the fall.

    Ⓐ leaves
    Ⓑ leafs
    Ⓒ leafes
    Ⓓ leafys

17. Which word belongs in the blank to complete this sentence?

    All the _____ houses were made of logs.

    Ⓐ settler
    Ⓑ settler's
    Ⓒ settlers'
    Ⓓ settlers's

18. Which word belongs in the blank to complete this sentence?

    I borrowed my _____ sweater to wear to school.

    Ⓐ mom
    Ⓑ mom's
    Ⓒ moms'
    Ⓓ moms's

19. Which is the correct abbreviation for the underlined word in this sentence?

    We drove down Commerce <u>Avenue</u> to get to the theater.

    Ⓐ A.
    Ⓑ An.
    Ⓒ Ane.
    Ⓓ Ave.

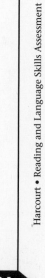

GO ON

Harcourt • Reading and Language Skills Assessment

LANGUAGE (continued)

20. Which is the correct abbreviation for the underlined word in this sentence?

My best friend is named Frank Garza, <u>Junior</u>.

Ⓐ Jan.

Ⓑ J.

Ⓒ Jr.

Ⓓ Jn.

21. What is the antecedent of the underlined word in this sentence?

Thelma sings well, but <u>she</u> could use some acting lessons.

Ⓐ Thelma

Ⓑ sings

Ⓒ acting

Ⓓ lessons

22. Which is the best pronoun to take the place of the underlined words in the sentence?

My friends are coming over, and <u>my friends</u> should arrive soon.

Ⓐ it

Ⓑ they

Ⓒ she

Ⓓ he

STOP

Make Yourself at Home / Theme 3
Reading and Language Skills Assessment

Orlando   Boston   Dallas   Chicago   San Diego

Part No. 9997-37749-4

ISBN 0-15-332203-9 (Package of 12)

TROPHIES

Reading and Language Skills Assessment Posttest

Lead the Way • Theme 3

Name _____ Date _____

SKILL AREA	Criterion Score	Pupil Score	Pupil Strength
COMPREHENSION			
Draw Conclusions	3/4	_____	_____
Compare and Contrast	6/8	_____	_____
LANGUAGE	7/10	_____	_____
Common and Proper Nouns			
Singular and Plural Nouns			
Possessive Nouns			
Abbreviations			
Pronouns and Antecedents			
TOTAL SCORE	16/22	_____	_____

Were accommodations made in administering this test? ☐ Yes ☐ No

Type of accommodations: _____

_____

COMPREHENSION: Draw Conclusions

Directions: Read the passage. Fill in the answer circle in front of the correct answer for each question.

One morning when I woke up, I heard a scratching sound outside my window. I knew there was a hole there, because my mother was planning to plant some flowers in that spot. I ran outside to see what was making the sound, and I found a little skunk! The skunk had probably gone into the hole to look for food, and then it could not climb out. It was very quiet.

I was not afraid, but I did not know how to help the skunk. My mother looked in our telephone directory and talked to people who knew how to help. She got a board and put it down into the hole. Then she said softly, "Kevin, let's move away and watch from a distance." After a short while, I smiled when I saw the skunk climb up the board and scamper away.

1. The skunk that Kevin found was probably a _____.
   Ⓐ pet animal
   Ⓑ wild animal
   Ⓒ farm animal
   Ⓓ circus animal

2. The skunk most likely went into the hole because it wanted to _____.
   Ⓐ get inside the house
   Ⓑ hide from Kevin
   Ⓒ find bugs to eat
   Ⓓ see some flowers

GO ON

COMPREHENSION: Draw Conclusions (continued)

3. How did Kevin most likely feel at the end of the story?

(A) upset

(B) happy

(C) angry

(D) bored

4. Kevin and his mother probably watched from a distance because they _____.

(A) did not want to frighten the skunk

(B) could see better from far away

(C) thought the skunk would hurt them

(D) did not care what the skunk would do

STOP

Harcourt • Reading and Language Skills Assessment

COMPREHENSION: Compare and Contrast

Directions: Read each passage. Fill in the answer circle in front of the correct answer for each question.

Wild lions and *domestic*, or tame, house cats are alike and different in many ways.

Both lions and house cats are blind and helpless when they are born. They depend on their mothers to give them milk and to protect them. When they get older, they both eat meat. They both have 30 teeth that they use to cut or tear chunks of meat to swallow whole. Neither lions nor house cats have teeth for chewing or grinding food.

One way lions and house cats are different is obvious—their size. Lions grow to be huge animals that can weigh from 250 to 500 pounds. Most cats weigh only about 5 to 15 pounds. A male lion can be 3 1/2 feet tall; an adult cat is usually about 10 inches tall. Both have fur, and it can be the same color. Only male lions, though, have manes.

Both house cats and lions move gracefully and are good hunters. They see well in dim light, and they have keen senses of smell and hearing. They are patient when they stalk their prey. They sneak up silently on padded feet. Then they pounce and use their claws to hold the prey. Lions can bring down large animals, such as antelopes or zebras. A house cat is more likely to catch a bird or a mouse.

5. One way lions and house cats are **alike** is that they both _____.
- Ⓐ hunt antelope
- Ⓑ are born blind
- Ⓒ are 3 1/2 feet tall
- Ⓓ weigh about 500 pounds

GO ON

COMPREHENSION: Compare and Contrast (continued)

6. One way lions are **different** from house cats is that only lions have _____.

Ⓐ fur

Ⓑ claws

Ⓒ 30 teeth

Ⓓ manes

7. **Neither** lions nor house cats have _____.

Ⓐ teeth for grinding food

Ⓑ keen hearing

Ⓒ good eyesight

Ⓓ keen sense of smell

8. Based on this passage, **both** house cats and lions can be described as _____.

Ⓐ huge

Ⓑ tame

Ⓒ graceful

Ⓓ slow

Harcourt • Reading and Language Skills Assessment

COMPREHENSION: Compare and Contrast (continued)

Sabrina and Matt are cousins. They both live near the Atlantic Ocean, but they live far from each other. Sabrina, who is ten, lives in Maine. Matt, who is nine, lives in Florida. They get to see each other every summer when their families get together for a visit in either Florida or Maine.

Where Sabrina lives, the ocean is cold. The shore is windy and rocky. Sabrina sits on the rocks, painting or writing. Waves crash against the rocks, making a loud roar. White sea foam splashes against the rocks. When Matt visits, Sabrina takes him walking and climbing along the shore. They listen to the waves and watch the fishing boats on the blue water.

Where Matt lives, the ocean is warm. The shore is a golden beach where Matt swims and plays volleyball. The waves roll gently onto the sand. When Sabrina visits Matt, they go for walks along the beach, looking for shells.

9. How are Sabrina and Matt **alike**?
- (A) They both live in Florida.
- (B) They are the same age.
- (C) They both live near the ocean.
- (D) They are brother and sister.

10. One way the ocean near Sabrina is **different** from the ocean near Matt is that the ocean near Sabrina has _____.
- (A) a rocky shore
- (B) gentle waves
- (C) golden sand
- (D) seashells

GO ON

Harcourt • Reading and Language Skills Assessment

COMPREHENSION: Compare and Contrast (continued)

11. In **both** places the children like to _____.
    - Ⓐ ride in a fishing boat
    - Ⓑ play in the sand
    - Ⓒ swim in the ocean
    - Ⓓ walk on the shore

12. The things Matt can do at the ocean are **different** from the things Sabrina can do, because the ocean where Matt lives is _____.
    - Ⓐ loud
    - Ⓑ warm
    - Ⓒ windy
    - Ⓓ foamy

STOP

Score _____

Harcourt • Reading and Language Skills Assessment

LANGUAGE

Directions: Read each sentence. Fill in the answer circle in front of the correct answer for each question.

13. Which word is a common noun in this sentence?

I definitely mailed my letter last Tuesday.

Ⓐ definitely

Ⓑ mailed

Ⓒ my

Ⓓ letter

14. Which word is a proper noun in this sentence?

We have an appointment with your teacher on Friday in the library.

Ⓐ appointment

Ⓑ teacher

Ⓒ Friday

Ⓓ library

15. Which word belongs in the blank to complete this sentence?

My favorite fruits are apples, grapes, and _____.

Ⓐ cherry

Ⓑ cherries

Ⓒ cherryes

Ⓓ cherrys

GO ON

Harcourt • Reading and Language Skills Assessment

LANGUAGE (continued)

16. Which word belongs in the blank to complete this sentence?

    Two of my _____ are loose.
    - Ⓐ tooth
    - Ⓑ tooths
    - Ⓒ toothes
    - Ⓓ teeth

17. Which word belongs in the blank to complete this sentence?

    All the _____ robes were made of red silk.
    - Ⓐ girl
    - Ⓑ girl's
    - Ⓒ girls'
    - Ⓓ girlses'

18. Which word belongs in the blank to complete this sentence?

    One _____ feathers were brightly colored.
    - Ⓐ bird's
    - Ⓑ birds'
    - Ⓒ birdses
    - Ⓓ birds's

19. Which is the correct abbreviation for the underlined word in this sentence?

    I put twelve <u>ounces</u> of cheese in the lasagna.
    - Ⓐ oc.
    - Ⓑ oz.
    - Ⓒ ouc.
    - Ⓓ ocs.

GO ON

Harcourt • Reading and Language Skills Assessment

LANGUAGE (continued)

20. Which is the correct abbreviation for the underlined word in this sentence?

    I am glad that <u>Doctor</u> Lowell will take care of me.

    Ⓐ Dec.

    Ⓑ Dtr.

    Ⓒ Dct.

    Ⓓ Dr.

21. What is the antecedent of the underlined word in this sentence?

    The teacher handed out the papers to the students in <u>her</u> class.

    Ⓐ teacher

    Ⓑ papers

    Ⓒ students

    Ⓓ class

22. Which is the best pronoun to take the place of the underlined words in the sentence?

    The students did a good job in the class play, and we clapped for <u>the students</u>.

    Ⓐ he

    Ⓑ she

    Ⓒ them

    Ⓓ it

STOP

· TROPHIES ·

Make Yourself at Home / Theme 3
Reading and Language Skills Assessment

Harcourt

Orlando   Boston   Dallas   Chicago   San Diego

Part No. 9997-37743-5

ISBN 0-15-332203-9 (Package of 12)

TROPHIES

Mid-Year Reading and Language Skills Assessment

Lead the Way • Themes 1, 2, 3

Name _____ Date _____

SKILL AREA	Criterion Score	Pupil Score	Pupil Strength
VOCABULARY	6/8	_____	_____
LITERARY RESPONSE AND ANALYSIS	4/6	_____	_____
COMPREHENSION	12/16	_____	_____
LANGUAGE	9/12	_____	_____
TOTAL SCORE	**31/42**	_____	_____

Were accommodations made in administering this test? ☐ Yes ☐ No

Type of accommodations: _____

_____

VOCABULARY

Directions: Read each sentence. Fill in the answer circle in front of the correct answer for each question.

1. It would be impossible to drive a car to the moon.

What does the word *impossible* mean?
- (A) possible before
- (B) not possible
- (C) possible again
- (D) wrongly possible

2. Which prefix can be added to the word *appear* to make it mean "appear again"?
- (A) super
- (B) dis
- (C) re
- (D) pre

3. Which prefix can be added to the word *loyal* to make it mean "not loyal"?
- (A) super
- (B) inter
- (C) multi
- (D) dis

4. The woman's face seemed to be ageless.

What does the word *ageless* mean?
- (A) able to age
- (B) filled with age
- (C) without age
- (D) characteristic of age

GO ON

VOCABULARY (continued)

5. **He is a famous sculptor.**

   What does the word *sculptor* mean?

   (A) able to sculpt

   (B) one who sculpts

   (C) without sculpting

   (D) relating to sculpting

6. Which suffix can be added to the word *flex* to make it mean "able to flex"?

   (A) ly

   (B) ful

   (C) ness

   (D) ible

7. Which word has the same root word as *automobile* and *autograph*?

   (A) autobiography

   (B) auditorium

   (C) authentic

   (D) august

8. Which word has the same root word as *microscope*?

   (A) midpoint

   (B) microphone

   (C) migration

   (D) milestone

STOP

Harcourt • Reading and Language Skills Assessment

LITERARY RESPONSE AND ANALYSIS

Directions: Read each passage. Then read the questions that follow each passage. Fill in the answer circle in front of the correct answer for each question.

It was a hot summer afternoon. The sun was like a giant fireball. Wanda was sitting on her front-porch swing. She was slowly swinging back and forth. The chain supporting the swing creaked each time the swing moved. Wanda was hot and bored. Her best friend, Sara, was gone for two weeks, so Wanda had no one to play with. She wished she could think of something to do for fun.

Just then Brad, Wanda's neighbor, came running up to the porch. "Wanda! Come on over to my house, quick! A lady just showed up with kittens to give away. If you hurry, you can choose a kitten to keep!"

"I'll be there in a minute," Wanda replied excitedly. "First I have to ask my mom if I can have one." She raced into the house to find her mother and ask permission. In a couple of minutes, Wanda hurried over to Brad's house. The lady with the kittens was still there. Wanda looked at the three kittens the lady had brought. She saw a furry lump of coal with green eyes looking up at her. She instantly fell in love with the little kitten and asked if she could have that one. The lady agreed, and Wanda took the kitten home. She knew she would not be bored now that she had a pet to keep her company.

LITERARY RESPONSE AND ANALYSIS (continued)

9. The main character in this story is _____.

Ⓐ Wanda's mom

Ⓑ Wanda

Ⓒ Sara

Ⓓ Brad

10. When does this story take place?

Ⓐ early in the morning

Ⓑ at lunchtime

Ⓒ during the afternoon

Ⓓ late at night

11. What is the problem in the story?

Ⓐ Wanda's friend Brad won't play with her.

Ⓑ Wanda is bored and needs something to do for fun.

Ⓒ Wanda and Brad need to earn money to buy a kitten.

Ⓓ Wanda argues with Sara just before Sara leaves for two weeks.

12. Which group of words in this story is a simile?

Ⓐ like a giant fireball

Ⓑ creaked each time

Ⓒ up to the porch

Ⓓ into the house

LITERARY RESPONSE AND ANALYSIS (continued)

13. How is the problem solved?

Ⓐ Wanda gets a new pet to keep her company.

Ⓑ Wanda gets a friendly letter from Sara.

Ⓒ Brad invites Wanda to play games at his house.

Ⓓ Mom gives Brad money for fixing the creaky porch swing.

14. Read this sentence from the story.

She saw a furry lump of coal with green eyes looking up at her.

Why does the author compare the kitten to coal?

Ⓐ because coal is hard and dry

Ⓑ because coal is a deep black color

Ⓒ because coal is powdery and messy

Ⓓ because coal is shaped like rocks

STOP

COMPREHENSION

Directions: Read each passage. Then read the questions that follow each passage. Fill in the answer circle in front of the correct answer for each question.

"I don't have a chance of winning the science poster contest," Jim moaned. "I can't think of anything flashy to put on my poster. Zack's father is in advertising. He'll probably help Zack do a fancy, slick-looking poster. Zack will win for sure."

"Just because Zack's father is in advertising doesn't mean Zack is going to win, Jim," his dad said. "I'm sure Zack's dad will tell him the same thing I'm going to tell you. Do your *own* work, do your *best* work, and keep in mind that winning isn't everything. Think about why you're making the poster in the first place."

Jim realized that his dad was right. He decided to forget about winning and just think about the reason for the poster contest—to persuade people to conserve natural resources. He made a list of all the ways his family could be less wasteful at home. They could turn off the water while they brushed their teeth. They could turn off lights when they left a room. They could wash their clothes in cold water and take faster showers. His list of ideas grew longer. Finally, he put a title on his poster: "Conservation Begins at Home."

The next day at the contest, the judge walked right past Zack's poster, but he stopped beside Jim's. He said, "Whoever made this poster put a lot of thought into it. There are some good ideas here for saving resources. This is just the sort of poster I was hoping to see, and this is the poster that wins first prize."

Harcourt • Reading and Language Skills Assessment

COMPREHENSION (continued)

15. Jim is afraid that when his poster is compared with Zack's, Zack's poster will _____.

Ⓐ have more conservation ideas

Ⓑ seem better researched

Ⓒ show more thought

Ⓓ look fancier

16. How does Jim's dad probably feel about the poster Jim makes?

Ⓐ disappointed that Jim didn't do a better job

Ⓑ worried that Jim doesn't know much about saving resources

Ⓒ proud that Jim put thought into his work

Ⓓ shocked that Jim thinks the family needs to save energy

17. Why is Jim's poster the kind the judge was hoping to see?

Ⓐ Jim's poster matches the reason for the contest.

Ⓑ Jim's poster is flashy and looks slick.

Ⓒ The judge was afraid no one would make a poster.

Ⓓ The judge couldn't understand the other posters.

18. Which statement is the best summary of this passage?

Ⓐ Jim worries that Zack will win the science poster contest because Zack's father is in advertising.

Ⓑ Jim forgets about trying to win a poster contest, thinks about the reason for making the poster in the first place, and wins first prize as a result.

Ⓒ Jim suggests that his family turn off the water when they brush their teeth.

Ⓓ Jim puts a title on his science poster: "Conservation Begins at Home."

GO ON

COMPREHENSION (continued)

Petroleum, a dark liquid that comes from the earth, is one of our most valuable resources. It has even been called "black gold." Some people call petroleum "crude oil." Thousands of products are made from petroleum. One of the most important of these products is gasoline. Gasoline is used to fuel our cars, trucks, trains, and airplanes. Oils and greases needed to make machines run smoothly are also made from petroleum. In fact, thousands of everyday products are made from materials found in petroleum. Cleaning fluids, laundry and dish detergents, rubber tires, asphalt for roofs and roads, printing ink, paint, and cosmetics all come from petroleum.

People have found uses for petroleum throughout history. More than 5,000 years ago, asphalt was used in Babylon to build walls and pave streets. Liquid oil was first used as a medicine by the ancient Egyptians. They also used *pitch*, which is natural asphalt, to coat some mummies. Oil products were also used to make weapons in the ancient world. During a battle as early as 480 B.C., the Persians used arrows dipped in oil-soaked fibers, which could be set on fire. American Indians used oil for medicines and for fuel. In the 1800s, some pioneers used oil as axle grease for their wagons. Some kerosene was made from petroleum, also. The kerosene was used to light lamps and lanterns.

COMPREHENSION (continued)

19. You can tell from this passage that petroleum _____.

Ⓐ has been replaced by man-made products

Ⓑ has been a valuable product for thousands of years

Ⓒ does not work as a source of fuel

Ⓓ is mostly used to make medicines

20. The Persians used oil on their arrows because the oil _____.

Ⓐ would burn

Ⓑ was poisonous

Ⓒ made the arrows fly faster

Ⓓ helped the arrows stick on the shaft

21. Both ancient Egyptians and American Indians used oil for _____.

Ⓐ axle grease

Ⓑ building walls

Ⓒ paving streets

Ⓓ medicines

22. It is likely that petroleum is called "black gold" because it _____.

Ⓐ is so valuable to people

Ⓑ is mostly used to make jewelry

Ⓒ looks like gold when the sun hits it

Ⓓ costs the same amount as gold to buy

GO ON

COMPREHENSION (continued)

Jan and her cousin Bess were spending a week at their aunt and uncle's farm in the country. They had just finished eating a huge breakfast. Next they were going to help Uncle Al do chores. Jan couldn't wait to help feed the pigs. However, she wanted to be polite and help her aunt first. "I'd be happy to wash the dishes for you," Jan offered.

"That would be a big help, Jan," Aunt Ann replied.

"I'm going to go on out to the pigpen," Bess said. She didn't want to do dishes.

After helping her aunt, Jan ran out to join Uncle Al and Bess. Al had saved some scraps for her to give the pigs. When the pigs were fed, Al, Bess, and Jan went to the henhouse. The two girls reached into the hens' nests and brought out large brown eggs. They gently put the eggs into a basket.

"I'd be happy to take the eggs back to the house," Jan told her uncle. "I think Aunt Ann needs them to bake a cake."

"That would be nice of you," Uncle Al replied.

Bess said, "I'm going to watch the horses." She didn't want to carry eggs anywhere.

After supper that night, Jan volunteered, "I'd be happy to clear the table for you, Aunt Ann."

Bess yawned and said, "I feel really sleepy. I'm going up to bed."

COMPREHENSION (continued)

23. At the beginning of the story, why does Jan offer to wash the dishes?

Ⓐ Uncle Al told her to help.

Ⓑ She wants to be polite.

Ⓒ She doesn't want to go feed the pigs.

Ⓓ She wants to make Bess look lazy.

24. Jan needs to take the eggs back to the house because _____.

Ⓐ the eggs will spoil outdoors

Ⓑ the pigs might try to eat the eggs

Ⓒ Aunt Ann needs the eggs for a cake

Ⓓ the hens will try to get their eggs back

25. At the end of the story, why does Bess yawn and say she is sleepy?

Ⓐ She is getting sick and weak.

Ⓑ She wants to go back out to feed the pigs.

Ⓒ She wants to go watch the horses again.

Ⓓ She doesn't want to help clear the table.

26. Compared with Bess, Jan is _____.

Ⓐ trickier

Ⓑ meaner

Ⓒ more helpful

Ⓓ more nervous

GO ON

COMPREHENSION (continued)

In 1607 three ships under the command of Captain Christopher Newport sailed to America. Some of the men on these ships were searching for treasure. Others were looking for land on which to grow farm products that could not be grown in England. The small group of about 100 men and boys sailed up the James River in Virginia. They started the first lasting English settlement in America—Jamestown. They named it in honor of King James of England.

They had not chosen the best place to settle. The land was swampy, the water was not clean, and mosquitoes carried diseases. Many of the colonists died of illness. Most of the settlers had been looking for gold rather than planning to farm the land. Thus, few of the settlers were willing or able to plant crops or build shelters. Captain John Smith managed to hold the colony together. He bought corn from the Indians and forced the settlers to work. Many disasters struck the colony, though. The settlers suffered through fire, drought, disease, and starvation. In 1610 new settlers and fresh supplies arrived to help keep the little colony going.

At first the colonists tried to grow crops that were not suited to the climate in Virginia. Later, though, they successfully raised hogs and Indian corn. In 1612 they began to grow a new type of tobacco. Tobacco, corn, and hogs helped the colony survive.

COMPREHENSION (continued)

27. According to the passage, the settlers at Jamestown suffered greatly because _____.

   Ⓐ there were many arguments over splitting up treasure

   Ⓑ the location of the settlement was not good

   Ⓒ too many men wanted to be in charge of the colony

   Ⓓ there were no trees to use for wood to build shelters

28. The colony of Jamestown survived because _____.

   Ⓐ the settlers learned to raise tobacco, corn, and hogs

   Ⓑ King James of England sent money to the colonists

   Ⓒ the settlers found a trade route to a nearby colony

   Ⓓ Christopher Newport taught the settlers to trade with the Indians

29. The first years of life for the settlers in Jamestown could best be described as _____.

   Ⓐ carefree

   Ⓑ harsh

   Ⓒ amusing

   Ⓓ mysterious

30. Which statement is the best summary of this passage?

   Ⓐ Some of the men on the three ships under the command of Captain Christopher Newport in 1607 were looking for treasure.

   Ⓑ The first colonists in Jamestown tried to grow crops that were not suited to the climate in Virginia.

   Ⓒ In 1607 Christopher Newport led a group of men and boys to found the first lasting English settlement in America at Jamestown, Virginia, and the colonists overcame many problems to survive.

   Ⓓ Many of the colonists in the first English settlement in America died of illness or of starvation.

STOP

LANGUAGE

Directions: Read each question. Fill in the answer circle in front of the correct answer for each question.

31. Which group of words is a sentence?

Ⓐ Excitedly opened the box.

Ⓑ The gentle, lapping waves.

Ⓒ The birds' songs were charming.

Ⓓ Climbed the steep mountain.

32. What kind of sentence is this?

Include a return envelope with your letter.

Ⓐ declarative

Ⓑ imperative

Ⓒ interrogative

Ⓓ exclamatory

33. Which answer best describes the underlined word in this sentence?

The sticky <u>honey</u> coated my fingers.

Ⓐ simple subject

Ⓑ simple predicate

Ⓒ compound subject

Ⓓ compound predicate

34. Which answer best describes the underlined words in this sentence?

The frogs <u>croaked and hopped</u> at the pond.

Ⓐ simple subject

Ⓑ simple predicate

Ⓒ compound subject

Ⓓ compound predicate

Harcourt • Reading and Language Skills Assessment

Lead the Way / Mid-Year Skills

LANGUAGE (continued)

35. Which answer best describes the underlined word in this sentence?

The roses and pansies <u>bloomed</u> with bright colors.

Ⓐ simple subject

Ⓑ simple predicate

Ⓒ compound subject

Ⓓ compound predicate

36. Which answer best describes the underlined words in this sentence?

<u>We raised the sail, and we glided on the water for hours.</u>

Ⓐ simple sentence

Ⓑ compound sentence

Ⓒ dependent clause

Ⓓ complex sentence

37. Which answer best describes the underlined words in this sentence?

<u>Because we were hungry,</u> we stopped for lunch.

Ⓐ simple sentence

Ⓑ compound sentence

Ⓒ dependent clause

Ⓓ complex sentence

38. Which word is a proper noun in this sentence?

The governor of Texas attended the opening of the new museum.

Ⓐ governor

Ⓑ Texas

Ⓒ opening

Ⓓ museum

GO ON

LANGUAGE (continued)

39. Which word belongs in the blank to complete this sentence?

Many _____ wore hats that had feathers or flowers attached.

Ⓐ lady

Ⓑ ladys

Ⓒ ladies

Ⓓ ladyes

40. Which word belongs in the blank to complete this sentence?

One _____ leaves were beginning to turn yellow.

Ⓐ trees'

Ⓑ trees's

Ⓒ tree

Ⓓ tree's

41. Which is the correct abbreviation for the underlined word in this sentence?

My uncle's office is on Pine <u>Street</u>.

Ⓐ S.

Ⓑ Srt.

Ⓒ St.

Ⓓ Strt.

42. What is the antecedent of the underlined word in this sentence?

My parents said I can sell cookies, but <u>they</u> want to talk to my scout troop leader about it.

Ⓐ parents

Ⓑ cookies

Ⓒ troop

Ⓓ leader

STOP

Score _____

Lead the Way / Mid-Year Skills

Harcourt • Reading and Language Skills Assessment

· T R O P H I E S ·

Lead the Way / Themes 1, 2, 3
Mid-Year Reading and Language Skills Assessment

Harcourt

Orlando   Boston   Dallas   Chicago   San Diego

Part No. 9997-37753-2

ISBN 0-15-332203-9 (Package of 12)

4

Reading and Language Skills
Assessment Pretest

Lead the Way • Theme 4

Name _____ Date _____

SKILL AREA	Criterion Score	Pupil Score	Pupil Strength
COMPREHENSION			
Main Idea and Details	3/4	_____	_____
Sequence	3/4	_____	_____
Follow Written Directions	3/4	_____	_____
LANGUAGE	7/10	_____	_____
Subject and Object Pronouns			
Possessive Pronouns			
Adjectives and Articles			
Comparing with Adjectives			
Verbs			
TOTAL SCORE	16/22	_____	_____

Were accommodations made in administering this test?   ❑ Yes   ❑ No

Type of accommodations: _____

_____

COMPREHENSION: Main Idea and Details

Directions: Read the passage. Fill in the answer circle in front of the correct answer for each question.

Air pollution has become a problem in many parts of our country today. When harmful substances end up in the air and make it unhealthful for us to breathe, we say that the air has become *polluted*.

Most air pollution results from human activities, but *pollutants* (substances that make the air unhealthful) can come from natural sources, too. A volcano, for example, can give off clouds of matter and gas that can harm living things. Dust storms and smoke from forest fires also pollute the air. Other natural pollutants include such things as pollen and bacteria.

Much of the man-made pollution in our country comes from vehicles, such as cars, trucks, buses, and airplanes. Other sources of man-made pollution are factories, power plants, furnaces, and the burning of garbage and other wastes.

Air pollution can be harmful to both humans and animals. It can lead to breathing difficulties and other health problems for both young and old.

1. What is the main idea of this passage?
   Ⓐ A volcano can give off clouds of matter and gas that can harm living things.
   Ⓑ Air pollution has become a problem in many parts of our country today.
   Ⓒ Other sources of man-made pollution are factories, power plants, furnaces, and the burning of garbage.
   Ⓓ Other natural pollutants include such things as dust, pollen, and bacteria.

GO ON

COMPREHENSION: Main Idea and Details (continued)

2. Which of these is a source of man-made air pollution?
   Ⓐ televisions
   Ⓑ books
   Ⓒ medicines
   Ⓓ trucks

3. Which of these is a source of natural air pollution?
   Ⓐ whales
   Ⓑ volcanoes
   Ⓒ rocks
   Ⓓ stars

4. According to the passage, air pollution can lead to _____.
   Ⓐ health problems
   Ⓑ forest fires
   Ⓒ dust storms
   Ⓓ bacteria growth

Score _____

Harcourt • Reading and Language Skills Assessment

COMPREHENSION: Sequence

Directions: Read the passage. Fill in the answer circle in front of the correct answer for each question.

I just had a really great weekend! When I woke up, I heard my dad say, "Luis, let's all go to the zoo. Your little sister can go in her stroller, and you and Mom and I will walk." Mom made us hot cereal for breakfast. After breakfast, while we were getting dressed, Dad said, "The weather is getting cool, and that's the best time to go to the zoo. The animals don't move around as much when it's hot."

Dad was right. It was a beautiful day, and the animals all seemed to be enjoying it. We hurried to see the lions. Then we went to see the tigers. After that we watched some polar bears, and then we saw some seals. My sister laughed at all the animals. Everything went fine until we got to the hippo. The hippo was in a pool, and we could stand up close and look right at it. It was enormous! My sister didn't like this animal. She pulled on Mom's sleeve and said, "Inside!" My sister doesn't know a lot of words yet, but we knew she wanted to get away from the hippo. So we pushed her stroller into the next building. But what a surprise—there was a huge hippo in there, too! Through a big pane of glass, we could see it swimming right toward us. This time my sister yelled, "Outside!" We got out of there in a hurry. Then Dad bought cotton candy for both of us, and my sister was happy again.

5. Which of these happened **first** after Luis woke up?

Ⓐ He ate hot cereal Mom made for breakfast.

Ⓑ He heard Dad say they were going to the zoo.

Ⓒ He put his sister in her stroller.

Ⓓ He began getting dressed.

GO ON

COMPREHENSION: Sequence (continued)

6. Which animals did the family see **just before** they saw the seals?

Ⓐ lions

Ⓑ hippos

Ⓒ tigers

Ⓓ polar bears

7. What did the family do **right after** Luis's sister said "Inside"?

Ⓐ They pushed her stroller into the next building.

Ⓑ They ate breakfast and got dressed.

Ⓒ They hurried to see the lions.

Ⓓ They walked to the zoo.

8. Which of these happened **last**?

Ⓐ Luis's sister yelled "Outside!"

Ⓑ A hippo swam toward the family.

Ⓒ Dad said, "The weather is getting cool."

Ⓓ Dad bought cotton candy for Luis and his sister.

Harcourt • Reading and Language Skills Assessment

COMPREHENSION: Follow Written Directions

Directions: Read the passage. Fill in the answer circle in front of the correct answer for each question.

It is easy to make blueberry muffins using a box mix. Here are the directions to follow.

Blueberry Muffins

Ingredients	Tools You Will Need
1 box of blueberry muffin mix	baking spray
1 egg	strainer
3/4 cup water	can opener
	small mixing bowl
	muffin tin with 12 cups
	large spoon

- Get out all the ingredients and tools you will need.
- Preheat the oven to 400°.
- Put baking spray into each muffin cup to keep the muffins from sticking.
- Open the can of blueberries that comes in the mix. Pour the berries into a strainer and rinse them with water.
- Put one egg and 3/4 cup of water into the mixing bowl. Blend together with the spoon.
- Add the muffin mix and stir until the egg, water, and mix are smooth.
- Add the strained blueberries to the batter and mix them in with the spoon.
- Spoon the batter into the greased muffin cups. Fill each cup about 3/4 full.
- Bake about 20 minutes or until golden brown.
- Let the muffins cool about 5 minutes before serving them.

GO ON

Harcourt • Reading and Language Skills Assessment

COMPREHENSION: Follow Written Directions (continued)

9. What do you use the strainer for?
   - Ⓐ to sift the muffin mix
   - Ⓑ to rinse the blueberries
   - Ⓒ to separate the egg
   - Ⓓ to measure the water

10. How much batter do you put in each muffin cup?
    - Ⓐ one spoonful
    - Ⓑ enough to reach the top
    - Ⓒ about 1/2 of the muffin cup
    - Ⓓ about 3/4 of the muffin cup

11. About how long do you bake the muffins?
    - Ⓐ 3 minutes
    - Ⓑ 4 minutes
    - Ⓒ 20 minutes
    - Ⓓ 400 minutes

12. What is the last step?
    - Ⓐ cool the muffins
    - Ⓑ preheat the oven
    - Ⓒ open the blueberries
    - Ⓓ get out the ingredients

Harcourt • Reading and Language Skills Assessment

LANGUAGE

Directions: Read each question. Fill in the answer circle in front of the correct answer for each question.

13. Which word is a subject pronoun in this sentence?

I think that Dad should grill out tonight.

Ⓐ I

Ⓑ think

Ⓒ Dad

Ⓓ grill

14. Which word is an object pronoun in this sentence?

Suzanne said that I could get the book from her.

Ⓐ Suzanne

Ⓑ get

Ⓒ book

Ⓓ her

15. Which pronoun correctly completes this sentence?

I brought my cap, and you brought _____.

Ⓐ my

Ⓑ yours

Ⓒ our

Ⓓ their

16. Which pronoun correctly completes this sentence?

Gene lets me borrow games that are _____.

Ⓐ his

Ⓑ my

Ⓒ your

Ⓓ our

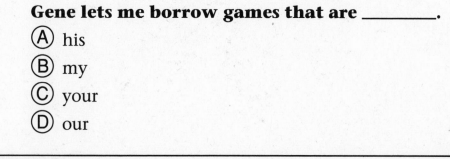

GO ON

LANGUAGE (continued)

---

17. Which word is an adjective in this sentence?

That tree has twisted branches.

(A) tree

(B) has

(C) twisted

(D) branches

18. Which word is an adjective in this sentence?

Some animals can go for days without water.

(A) Some

(B) animals

(C) go

(D) water

19. Which word is an article in this sentence?

Maria decorated colorful eggs for the fiesta.

(A) Maria

(B) decorated

(C) eggs

(D) the

20. Which adjective correctly completes this sentence?

This door is _____ than that one.

(A) more wider

(B) wider

(C) most widest

(D) widest

Harcourt • Reading and Language Skills Assessment

LANGUAGE (continued)

21. Which word is the action verb in this sentence?

We packed several bags for the long trip.

Ⓐ We

Ⓑ packed

Ⓒ bags

Ⓓ long

22. Which word is the verb that shows being in this sentence?

All the animals in the zoo are healthy.

Ⓐ animals

Ⓑ zoo

Ⓒ are

Ⓓ healthy

STOP

· TROPHIES ·

Creative Minds / Theme 4
Reading and Language Skills Assessment

Harcourt

Orlando   Boston   Dallas   Chicago   San Diego

Part No. 9997-37750-8

ISBN 0-15-332203-9 (Package of 12)

4

Reading and Language Skills Assessment Posttest

Lead the Way • Theme 4

Name _____ Date _____

SKILL AREA	Criterion Score	Pupil Score	Pupil Strength
COMPREHENSION			
Main Idea and Details	3/4	_____	_____
Sequence	3/4	_____	_____
Follow Written Directions	3/4	_____	_____
LANGUAGE Subject and Object Pronouns Possessive Pronouns Adjectives and Articles Comparing with Adjectives Verbs	7/10	_____	_____
TOTAL SCORE	16/22	_____	_____

Were accommodations made in administering this test? ❑ Yes ❑ No

Type of accommodations: _____

_____

COMPREHENSION: Main Idea and Details

Railroads played an important part in helping the ranching industry in Texas to grow. In the early 1800s, there was not a lot of money to be made from raising cattle in Texas. Ranchers at that time raised cattle mostly for leather and for fat, which they used to make candles and soap. Later, people in cities in the East became eager to buy beef, and they were willing to pay a lot of money to get it. Ranchers could get ten times as much money for their cattle in the East as they could get in Texas. However, they had no good way to get the cattle from Texas to the cities in the East.

Railroads helped the ranchers by providing a way to get Texas cattle to distant markets. Ranchers began to organize cattle drives along trails that led from Texas through Oklahoma and north to "cow towns." The cow towns were places where *stockyards*, or cattle pens, were built near railroad lines. When the herds reached the stockyards, they could be loaded into railroad cars. The railroad cars could then carry the cattle to markets in the East.

1. What is this passage mostly about?
   Ⓐ how to build and operate a railroad
   Ⓑ how railroads helped Texas cattle ranchers
   Ⓒ future plans for railroads in Texas
   Ⓓ how to make candles and soap from beef fat

2. Ranchers wanted to sell their cattle in the East because _____.
   Ⓐ people in the East would pay more for beef
   Ⓑ no one in Texas would buy beef
   Ⓒ in Texas, beef could only be used to make leather
   Ⓓ they wanted to help the railroads make money

GO ON

COMPREHENSION: Main Idea and Details (continued)

3. Ranchers organized cattle drives to _____.
   Ⓐ move cattle to warmer places for the winter
   Ⓑ bring new breeds of cattle from the East back to Texas
   Ⓒ get their cattle to stockyards near railroads
   Ⓓ keep cattle moving so they could not be stolen

4. Cow towns were important to ranchers because the cow towns _____.
   Ⓐ had cattle pens built near railroads
   Ⓑ were all located in the East
   Ⓒ had the best grazing land for cattle
   Ⓓ were the best place to get supplies for cattle drives

STOP

Harcourt • Reading and Language Skills Assessment

COMPREHENSION: Sequence

Directions: Read the passage. Fill in the answer circle in front of the correct answer for each question.

One day a little girl named Blue Sky lived in America—perhaps before the Europeans came. Blue Sky wanted to make a bowl to hold water. She asked her mother how to make the bowl, and her mother said, "This is what you must do. First, dig some clay from the ground. Next, soak the clay in water to soften it, and be sure to keep the clay soft and wet. After that, roll the clay in your hands to make a big, smooth ball. Then put your fist right into the middle of the ball. Make the bottom flat, and that will make a bowl. If you want to, you can paint designs on your bowl. Then you must let the bowl dry. When your bowl is dry, it will be good to hold nuts and berries, but not water. The bowl will not keep its shape if it gets wet. To hold water, the bowl must be baked."

Blue Sky did everything her mother told her. She dug clay, shaped it, and painted designs on it. Soon she had a lovely bowl decorated with stars and moons around the outside. She still needed to bake, or fire, the bowl, though. Her mother told her that to fire the bowl, they would have to wait for a clear, dry day with little wind. They waited for several days, and then they fired the bowl. About a week after Blue Sky had dug the clay, she had a beautiful water bowl to drink from. She filled the bowl with clear, cool water from a nearby stream and took a long drink.

5. Which of these happened **first** in the passage?
- Ⓐ Blue Sky painted designs on her bowl.
- Ⓑ Blue Sky asked her mother how to make a bowl.
- Ⓒ Blue Sky had a beautiful water bowl to drink from.
- Ⓓ Blue Sky and her mother waited for a clear, dry day.

GO ON ▶

COMPREHENSION: Sequence (continued)

6. What did Blue Sky do **just before** she made the bottom of the clay flat?
   (A) fired the clay
   (B) let the clay dry
   (C) put her fist into the clay
   (D) painted designs on the clay

7. What did Blue Sky do **just after** she painted designs on the bowl?
   (A) rolled the clay in her hands
   (B) soaked the clay in water
   (C) fired the bowl
   (D) let the bowl dry

8. Which of these happened **last** in the passage?
   (A) Blue Sky fired her bowl.
   (B) Blue Sky drank from her bowl.
   (C) Blue Sky dug clay from the ground.
   (D) Blue Sky painted stars and moons on her bowl.

Harcourt • Reading and Language Skills Assessment

Score _____

COMPREHENSION: Follow Written Directions

Directions: Read the passage. Fill in the answer circle in front of the correct answer for each question.

When Leon's friend Anna sprained her ankle, these instructions told him how to help Anna.

How to Treat a Sprained Ankle

1. *Rest*. Stay off the foot and rest it.

2. *Ice*. Use ice to keep the ankle from swelling. Wrap a soft cloth around a bag of ice and put it on the injured ankle. Keep the ice in place for about ten to fifteen minutes.

3. *Compress*. Wrap an elastic bandage around the injured ankle to reduce swelling. Make the bandage snug, but do not wrap it so tightly that it cuts off circulation. If toes begin to tingle, the bandage is too tight. Loosen it a little to help the blood flow freely.

4. *Elevate*. Prop the injured ankle up on pillows. Keeping the ankle above the level of the heart will help reduce swelling and pain.

If the ankle continues to be painful, see a doctor. The doctor can make sure that no bones are broken or cracked and can decide whether the sprain needs more treatment.

Harcourt • Reading and Language Skills Assessment

GO ON

COMPREHENSION: Follow Written Directions (continued)

9. What do the instructions say Leon should do first?
   Ⓐ have Anna sit down to rest her foot
   Ⓑ prop Anna's ankle up on pillows
   Ⓒ check to see whether Anna's toes are tingling
   Ⓓ wrap a bandage tightly around Anna's ankle

10. What is ice used for?
    Ⓐ to keep Anna's ankle firmly in place
    Ⓑ to keep Anna's ankle from swelling
    Ⓒ to keep Anna's ankle from hurting
    Ⓓ to keep Anna's ankle from bleeding

11. How long should Leon keep the ice in place?
    Ⓐ about 5 minutes
    Ⓑ about 10 to 15 minutes
    Ⓒ about 30 minutes
    Ⓓ until Anna goes to the doctor

12. You need pillows for step _____.
    Ⓐ 1
    Ⓑ 2
    Ⓒ 3
    Ⓓ 4

LANGUAGE

Directions: Read each question. Fill in the answer circle in front of the correct answer for each question.

13. Which word is a subject pronoun in this sentence?

They searched high and low for the lost library book.
Ⓐ They
Ⓑ searched
Ⓒ lost
Ⓓ book

14. Which word is an object pronoun in this sentence?

The guests aren't here yet, but those cookies are for them.
Ⓐ guests
Ⓑ aren't
Ⓒ cookies
Ⓓ them

15. Which pronoun correctly completes this sentence?

Ed will get his swim suit, and I already have _____ on.
Ⓐ our
Ⓑ mine
Ⓒ my
Ⓓ their

16. Which pronoun correctly completes this sentence?

My sister gave me all the clothes that are _____.
Ⓐ your
Ⓑ their
Ⓒ hers
Ⓓ our

GO ON

LANGUAGE (continued)

17. Which word is an adjective in this sentence?

The Millers prepare Italian food frequently.

Ⓐ Millers

Ⓑ prepare

Ⓒ Italian

Ⓓ food

18. Which word is an adjective in this sentence?

Many stars are hidden by the clouds.

Ⓐ Many

Ⓑ stars

Ⓒ are

Ⓓ clouds

19. Which word is an article in this sentence?

I would like an apple, please.

Ⓐ I

Ⓑ like

Ⓒ an

Ⓓ apple

20. Which adjective correctly completes this sentence?

Which of the four pies is the _____?

Ⓐ sweeter

Ⓑ sweetest

Ⓒ more sweeter

Ⓓ most sweetest

Harcourt • Reading and Language Skills Assessment

LANGUAGE (continued)

21. Which word is the action verb in this sentence?

    The lion chased a large antelope through the tall grass.

    (A) chased

    (B) antelope

    (C) tall

    (D) grass

22. Which word is the verb that shows being in this sentence?

    That gown is my sister's wedding dress.

    (A) gown

    (B) is

    (C) sister's

    (D) dress

STOP

· TROPHIES ·

Creative Minds / Theme 4
Reading and Language Skills Assessment

◤Harcourt

Orlando   Boston   Dallas   Chicago   San Diego

Part No. 9997-37744-3

ISBN 0-15-332203-9 (Package of 12)

4

TROPHIES

Reading and Language Skills
Assessment Pretest

Lead the Way • Theme 5

Name _____ Date _____

SKILL AREA	Criterion Score	Pupil Score	Pupil Strength
COMPREHENSION			
Author's Purpose	3/4	_____	_____
Elements of Nonfiction	3/4	_____	_____
RESEARCH AND INFORMATION SKILLS			
Reference Sources	3/4	_____	_____
LANGUAGE	7/10	_____	_____
Main and Helping Verbs			
Action and Linking Verbs			
Present Tense			
Past and Future Tenses			
Irregular Verbs			
TOTAL SCORE	16/22	_____	

Were accommodations made in administering this test?   ☐ Yes   ☐ No

Type of accommodations: _____

_____

ISBN 0-15-332203-9

10   170   10 09 08 07 06 05

COMPREHENSION: Author's Purpose and Perspective

Directions: Read each passage. Fill in the answer circle in front of the correct answer for each question.

Author 1

The Statue of Liberty is a large statue that stands in New York Harbor. France gave the statue to the United States in 1884 as a symbol of friendship and of the freedom that citizens enjoy under our form of government.

The statue shows a proud woman dressed in a loose robe. Her right arm holds a great torch raised high in the air. Her left arm holds a tablet bearing the date of the Declaration of Independence. On her head is a crown of spikes, like huge rays of the sun. At her feet is a broken shackle, which stands for the overthrowing of tyranny.

At the base of the statue is a poem, "The New Colossus," written by Emma Lazarus. The poem tells how the Statue of Liberty welcomes immigrants to America.

Author 2

There are many wonderful sights to see in New York, but there is only one sight that you really *must* see—the Statue of Liberty. It is one of the most beautiful sights in the world. So many times I have heard my grandmother tell about the first time she saw the statue when she and her family came to the United States to live. She said she knew that it meant they were welcome in America—land of the free.

The statue has welcomed many, many immigrants to our country. To people who may have left their homelands because of war, hunger, or fear, the statue is a symbol of hope, freedom, and a new chance at a good life. This is why you really *must* go to see the Statue of Liberty.

GO ON

COMPREHENSION: Author's Purpose and Perspective (continued)

1. The main purpose of Author 1 is to _____.
   - (A) inform
   - (B) persuade
   - (C) entertain
   - (D) warn

2. Which of the following statements would most likely be used by Author 1?
   - (A) The Statue of Liberty is the most beautiful sight in the entire world.
   - (B) The Statue of Liberty stands 151 feet high and weighs about 450,000 pounds.
   - (C) No other sight in America could ever mean as much to visitors as the Statue of Liberty.
   - (D) The Statue of Liberty rises tall and proud and must never be removed because it is a symbol of hope for so many.

3. The main purpose of Author 2 is to _____.
   - (A) inform
   - (B) persuade
   - (C) entertain
   - (D) warn

4. With which statement would Author 2 most likely agree?
   - (A) The Statue of Liberty stands for all the hopes and dreams of people who first come to America.
   - (B) The Statue of Liberty serves no purpose but looks pretty.
   - (C) The Statue of Liberty should be moved out of New York Harbor.
   - (D) The Statue of Liberty costs too much to maintain and should be taken down.

STOP

Score _____

Harcourt • Reading and Language Skills Assessment

COMPREHENSION: Elements of Nonfiction

Directions: Read each passage. Fill in the answer circle in front of the correct answer for each question.

A Land of Fire and Ice

Would you like to visit a land where you can see things that are very hot and very cold? If you visited Iceland, you would be in a country that has both volcanoes and glaciers. That is why the country is called the "Land of Fire and Ice."

Facts About Iceland

Iceland has hot springs and volcanoes. In this small area, a volcano erupts about every five years! There are about 200 volcanoes in Iceland. It is one of the most active volcano areas in the world.

Much of Iceland is covered with the sparkling ice of glaciers. The third largest glacier in the world is located in Iceland.

5. This passage is mainly organized by _____.
   Ⓐ cause and effect
   Ⓑ main idea and details
   Ⓒ sequence of events
   Ⓓ comparison and contrast

6. What purpose does the phrase **Facts About Iceland** serve in this passage?
   Ⓐ It is the title of the passage.
   Ⓑ It is a caption for an illustration.
   Ⓒ It is a heading that tells what a section will be about.
   Ⓓ It is the topic sentence of the second paragraph.

GO ON ▶

COMPREHENSION: Elements of Nonfiction (continued)

Going North

Matthew Henson (1866–1955), an African American explorer from Maryland, began having world adventures as a teenager. That is when he spent six years as a sailor. In those six years, he sailed all around the world.

Then, in 1888, Henson joined Admiral Robert Peary for the first of their many explorations together. The first trip took them to Nicaragua. A few years later, Henson and Peary changed direction—they took their first trip to find the North Pole.

Matthew Henson worked hard to help them find their way. He learned the language of the Inuit, or Eskimo, so that he could talk with them. Finally, in 1909, Matthew Henson and Robert Peary reached the North Pole.

In 1944 Henson took another trip. He went to Washington, D.C., to receive a medal for his important work.

---

7. This passage is mainly organized by _____.
   Ⓐ cause and effect
   Ⓑ main idea and details
   Ⓒ sequence of events
   Ⓓ comparison and contrast

8. What purpose does the phrase **Going North** serve in this passage?
   Ⓐ It is the title of the passage.
   Ⓑ It is a caption for an illustration.
   Ⓒ It is a heading that tells what a section will be about.
   Ⓓ It is the topic sentence of the first paragraph.

Score _____   *Lead the Way / Theme 5*

Harcourt • Reading and Language Skills Assessment

RESEARCH AND INFORMATION SKILLS: Reference Sources

Directions: Fill in the answer circle in front of the **best** answer for each question.

9. Where would you look to find a synonym for the word *uncomfortable*?
   Ⓐ thesaurus
   Ⓑ encyclopedia
   Ⓒ almanac
   Ⓓ atlas

10. What would be the **best** source of information for a report on eagles?
   Ⓐ atlas
   Ⓑ dictionary
   Ⓒ encyclopedia
   Ⓓ newspaper

11. Where would you look to find out how much the cost of an average restaurant meal changed from 2000–2001?
   Ⓐ encyclopedia
   Ⓑ almanac
   Ⓒ dictionary
   Ⓓ thesaurus

12. Where would you look to find a synonym for the word *exciting*?
   Ⓐ atlas
   Ⓑ almanac
   Ⓒ thesaurus
   Ⓓ encyclopedia

STOP

LANGUAGE

Directions: Read each question. Fill in the answer circle in front of the correct answer for each question.

13. Which word is the main verb in this sentence?

    I could hear a bell in the distance.

    Ⓐ could

    Ⓑ hear

    Ⓒ bell

    Ⓓ in

14. Which word is the helping verb in this sentence?

    Jade has completed all her homework.

    Ⓐ has

    Ⓑ completed

    Ⓒ her

    Ⓓ homework

15. Which word is the action verb in this sentence?

    The polar bear moved quickly across the ice.

    Ⓐ bear

    Ⓑ moved

    Ⓒ across

    Ⓓ ice

16. Which word is the linking verb in this sentence?

    That tall girl is my cousin.

    Ⓐ tall

    Ⓑ girl

    Ⓒ is

    Ⓓ my

Harcourt • Reading and Language Skills Assessment

GO ON

Lead the Way / Theme 5

LANGUAGE (continued)

17. Which present-tense verb agrees with the subject in this sentence?

He eats a snack and _____ television.

Ⓐ watched

Ⓑ will watch

Ⓒ watch

Ⓓ watches

18. Which present-tense verb agrees with the subject in this sentence?

Now the hungry wolf _____ the field and sees something to eat.

Ⓐ will search

Ⓑ searched

Ⓒ searches

Ⓓ search

19. Which is the correct past-tense verb to complete this sentence?

Yesterday Mom _____ my brother's soccer game.

Ⓐ film

Ⓑ films

Ⓒ filmed

Ⓓ will film

20. Which answer shows the future-tense verb needed to complete this sentence?

Next weekend we _____ out the garage.

Ⓐ clean

Ⓑ cleans

Ⓒ cleaned

Ⓓ will clean

GO ON

LANGUAGE (continued)

21. Which is the correct verb form to complete this sentence?

I thought I _____ the answer, but I was wrong.

Ⓐ knew

Ⓑ knowed

Ⓒ knows

Ⓓ know

22. Which is the correct verb form to complete this sentence?

Last week my uncle _____ my cousin and me to a theme park.

Ⓐ taked

Ⓑ took

Ⓒ take

Ⓓ takes

STOP

Score _____

Lead the Way / Theme 5

Harcourt • Reading and Language Skills Assessment

· TROPHIES ·

Community Ties / Theme 5
Reading and Language Skills Assessment

Harcourt

Orlando   Boston   Dallas   Chicago   San Diego

Part No. 9997-37751-6

ISBN 0-15-332203-9 (Package of 12)

4

TROPHIES

Reading and Language Skills Assessment Posttest

Lead the Way • Theme 5

Name _____ Date _____

SKILL AREA	Criterion Score	Pupil Score	Pupil Strength
COMPREHENSION			
Author's Purpose	3/4	_____	_____
Elements of Nonfiction	3/4	_____	_____
RESEARCH AND INFORMATION SKILLS			
Reference Sources	3/4	_____	_____
LANGUAGE	7/10	_____	_____
Main and Helping Verbs			
Action and Linking Verbs			
Present Tense			
Past and Future Tenses			
Irregular Verbs			
TOTAL SCORE	16/22	_____	_____

Were accommodations made in administering this test? ❑ Yes ❑ No

Type of accommodations: _____

_____

COMPREHENSION: Author's Purpose and Perspective

Directions: Read each passage. Fill in the answer circle in front of the correct answer for each question.

Author 1

An interesting battle in nature is the never-ending conflict between ants and ant lions. Ant lions are the larval stage of insects that look like dragonflies. Sometimes they are called "doodlebugs." Doodlebugs are unlike other insects because they walk backward almost all the time. The bug walks carefully backward in a spiral, or round and round, pattern until it has built a funnel in very fine dirt or sand. Then the ant lion hides in the bottom of the funnel, waiting for an ant to fall in. When an ant falls in, the ant lion reaches out with two large jaws that clamp together like the pincers of a lobster. Usually any ant colony nearby soon figures out that ant lions are close and moves away—or at least avoids the funnels. Then the little doodlebugs just move on to where the ants have built their new homes.

Author 2

If you have never watched doodlebugs, or ant lions, trying to catch ants, you ought to start now. Nothing is more fun than watching doodlebugs trying to catch ants! All you have to do is sit or lie beside a doodlebug den, watch closely, and wait. Most people think of exciting battles going on between large animals such as lions and antelopes. But the battles in the insect world are just as exciting, and much easier to see up close. Start watching ant lions!

GO ON

COMPREHENSION: Author's Purpose and Perspective (continued)

1. The main purpose of Author 1 is to _____.
   - (A) persuade
   - (B) inform
   - (C) entertain
   - (D) warn

2. Which of the following sentences would most likely be used by Author 1?
   - (A) The ant lion lies in wait to catch the insects on which it feeds.
   - (B) It's great fun to see an ant lion come out and shake his jaws at you.
   - (C) For even more fun, tickle an ant lion's funnel to get the ant lion to come out.
   - (D) It's easy to watch doodlebugs, and you're going to like it.

3. The main purpose of Author 2 is to _____.
   - (A) persuade
   - (B) inform
   - (C) entertain
   - (D) warn

4. Which of the following sentences would most likely be used by Author 2?
   - (A) The ant lion has a pair of sword-shaped jaws.
   - (B) The ant lion usually chooses dry, sandy soil for its pit.
   - (C) Your friends will like to watch the ant lions, too!
   - (D) An ant lion pit sometimes reaches two inches across.

STOP

Score _____

Harcourt • Reading and Language Skills Assessment

COMPREHENSION: Elements of Nonfiction

Directions: Read each passage. Fill in the answer circle in front of the correct answer for each question.

THE GRAND CANYON

The Grand Canyon has been called one of the seven wonders of the world. Carved by the Colorado River, the Grand Canyon is widely known for its beautiful scenery.

Description of the Canyon

The canyon walls have been formed into fanciful shapes. They are striped with colors, from pinks and greens to red, brown, gray, and even violet. The gorge itself is 277 miles long and a mile deep.

The Cliff Walls

The cliff walls contain a history of the earth. There are fossils pressed into the rock. They show the remains of reptiles and insects.

5. This passage is mainly organized by _____.
   - (A) cause and effect
   - (B) main idea and details
   - (C) sequence of events
   - (D) comparison and contrast

6. Which information would you expect to find in the section **Description of the Canyon?**
   - (A) The canyon is 18 miles across at its widest point.
   - (B) Fossils on the cliff walls show how the earth has changed.
   - (C) Some fossils on the walls show the remains of seashells.
   - (D) Even rain and wind have left their marks on the cliff walls.

GO ON

COMPREHENSION: Elements of Nonfiction (continued)

BEARS

The Alaskan brown bear is the largest meat-eating animal that lives on land. This kind of bear can grow to be about 9 feet long. It can weigh up to 1,700 pounds! By contrast, the sun bear, which is also known as the Malayan bear, is the smallest kind of bear. It is about 3 to 4 feet long, and it weighs only about 60 to 100 pounds.

Where the Bears Live

Alaskan brown bears are usually found on the mainland of Alaska and on other Alaskan islands, such as Kodiak Island off the southeastern coast of the state.

Sun bears live in the forests of Borneo, Burma, Indochina, the Malay Peninsula, and other areas. They bend the branches of trees to make nests or beds to sleep in during the day.

How They Look

The color of the Alaskan brown bear can vary from yellowish to nearly black. Most sun bears have a black coat.

7. This passage is mainly organized by _____.
- Ⓐ cause and effect
- Ⓑ main idea and details
- Ⓒ sequence of events
- Ⓓ comparison and contrast

8. What purpose does the phrase **Where the Bears Live** serve in this passage?
- Ⓐ It is the title of the passage.
- Ⓑ It is a caption for an illustration.
- Ⓒ It is a heading that tells what a section will be about.
- Ⓓ It is the topic sentence of the second paragraph.

STOP

Score _____ *Lead the Way / Theme 5*

RESEARCH AND INFORMATION SKILLS: Reference Sources

Directions: Fill in the answer circle in front of the best answer for each question.

9. Where would you look to find a synonym for the word *swift*?
Ⓐ thesaurus
Ⓑ encyclopedia
Ⓒ almanac
Ⓓ atlas

10. Where would you look to find information for a report on Spain?
Ⓐ dictionary
Ⓑ thesaurus
Ⓒ encyclopedia
Ⓓ newspaper

11. Where would you look to find what states Lake Superior touches?
Ⓐ telephone directory
Ⓑ dictionary
Ⓒ thesaurus
Ⓓ atlas

12. Where could you find a list of weather forecasts for the year?
Ⓐ atlas
Ⓑ almanac
Ⓒ dictionary
Ⓓ encyclopedia

STOP

LANGUAGE

Directions: Read each question. Fill in the answer circle in front of the correct answer for each question.

13. Which word is the main verb in this sentence?

The students will elect a class president.

(A) students

(B) will

(C) elect

(D) president

14. Which word is the helping verb in this sentence?

Everyone should protect our natural resources.

(A) Everyone

(B) should

(C) protect

(D) our

15. Which word is the action verb in this sentence?

The lion crouched in the tall, thick grass.

(A) lion

(B) crouched

(C) tall

(D) grass

16. Which word is the linking verb in this sentence?

The guest speaker seems nervous.

(A) guest

(B) speaker

(C) seems

(D) nervous

Harcourt • Reading and Language Skills Assessment

GO ON

Lead the Way / Theme 5

LANGUAGE (continued)

17. Which present-tense verb agrees with the subject in this sentence?

Now the bear _____ in the stream and catches his dinner.

Ⓐ fish

Ⓑ fished

Ⓒ will fish

Ⓓ fishes

18. Which present-tense verb agrees with the subject in this sentence?

Today many people _____ microwaves to cook with.

Ⓐ has

Ⓑ have

Ⓒ had

Ⓓ will have

19. Which is the correct past-tense verb to complete this sentence?

Yesterday I _____ everyone when I hit a home run.

Ⓐ amazed

Ⓑ amaze

Ⓒ amazes

Ⓓ will amaze

20. Which answer shows the future-tense verb needed to complete this sentence?

Tomorrow class members _____ their stories.

Ⓐ share

Ⓑ shares

Ⓒ shared

Ⓓ will share

GO ON

LANGUAGE (continued)

21. Which is the correct verb form to complete this sentence?

Our class has _____ a group science project.

Ⓐ begun

Ⓑ beginned

Ⓒ began

Ⓓ begins

22. Which is the correct verb form to complete this sentence?

I have already _____ the dog a bath.

Ⓐ gived

Ⓑ given

Ⓒ gave

Ⓓ gives

STOP

Score _____

· T R O P H I E S ·

Community Ties / Theme 5
Reading and Language Skills Assessment

Harcourt

Orlando   Boston   Dallas   Chicago   San Diego

Part No. 9997-37745-1

ISBN 0-15-332203-9 (Package of 12)

TROPHIES

Reading and Language Skills
Assessment Pretest

Lead the Way • Theme 6

Name _____ Date _____

SKILL AREA	Criterion Score	Pupil Score	Pupil Strength
VOCABULARY Word Relationships	3/4	_____	_____
COMPREHENSION Fact and Opinion	3/4	_____	_____
Paraphrase	3/4	_____	_____
LANGUAGE Contractions and Negatives Adverbs Comparing with Adverbs Prepositions Prepositional Phrases	7/10	_____	_____
TOTAL SCORE	16/22	_____	_____

Were accommodations made in administering this test? ☐ Yes ☐ No

Type of accommodations: _____

_____

VOCABULARY: Word Relationships

Directions: Fill in the answer circle in front of the correct answer for each question.

1. Read this sentence.

I put the empty box beneath the stairs.

Which word means about the **same** thing as *beneath*?
(A) on
(B) near
(C) under
(D) around

2. Read this sentence.

That girl is a swift runner.

Which word means the **opposite** of *swift*?
(A) new
(B) slow
(C) tired
(D) strong

3. How are the words *real* and *reel* related?
(A) They are synonyms.
(B) They are antonyms.
(C) They are homophones.
(D) They are homographs.

4. How are the words *many* and *several* related?
(A) They are synonyms.
(B) They are antonyms.
(C) They are homophones.
(D) They are homographs.

STOP

Harcourt • Reading and Language Skills Assessment

COMPREHENSION: Fact and Opinion

Directions: Read the passage. Fill in the answer circle in front of the correct answer for each question.

Most people dislike skunks. That is because skunks give off an unpleasant odor. Skunks are members of the weasel family. Weasels are unpopular animals, also. It is not surprising to learn that skunks and weasels are in the same family.

Skunks are strange-looking animals. They are about the size of a large house cat, and they have black-and-white markings. The white fur on a skunk's forehead and back looks exactly as if someone painted a stripe right down its back. The skunk has an arched back, a broad forehead, and short legs. It moves rather slowly. A skunk looks silly when it walks.

A skunk has a pair of glands near its tail. When a skunk is frightened, these glands can give out a bad-smelling fluid to help defend it from its enemies. A skunk can shoot the fluid as far as ten feet into the air. The glands can be removed, and then skunks make the best pets in the world. Everyone should have a pet skunk at least once!

Skunks sleep during the day and come out at night. All farmers love skunks. This is because skunks eat insects, rats, mice, and other small animals that can hurt crops. Skunks also eat eggs, though, so they are not so helpful to farmers raising hens.

5. Which of the following is a **fact** from the passage?
   Ⓐ Most people dislike skunks.
   Ⓑ Weasels are unpopular animals.
   Ⓒ It is not surprising to learn that skunks and weasels are in the same family.
   Ⓓ The skunk has an arched back, a broad forehead, and short legs.

New Lands / Theme 6

Harcourt • Reading and Language Skills Assessment

COMPREHENSION: Fact and Opinion (continued)

6. Which of the following is an **opinion** from the passage?
- Ⓐ Skunks sleep during the day and come out at night.
- Ⓑ Skunks make the best pets in the world.
- Ⓒ Skunks eat insects, rats, mice, and other small animals.
- Ⓓ Skunks also eat eggs.

7. Which of the following is a **fact** from the passage?
- Ⓐ Everyone should have a pet skunk at least once!
- Ⓑ A skunk looks silly when it walks.
- Ⓒ Skunks are members of the weasel family.
- Ⓓ All farmers love skunks.

8. Which of the following is an **opinion** from the passage?
- Ⓐ Skunks have black-and-white markings.
- Ⓑ A skunk has a pair of glands near its tail.
- Ⓒ The glands can be removed.
- Ⓓ Skunks are strange-looking animals.

STOP

COMPREHENSION: Paraphrase

Directions: Read the passage. Fill in the answer circle in front of the correct answer for each question.

Patrick wanted to win the school spelling bee more than anything. He had been practicing for weeks, looking up words in the dictionary and spelling them out loud until he knew them by heart. He knew, though, that his best friend, Melissa Sanchez, would provide stiff competition. Melissa seemed able to spell any word without even having to study.

Finally the day of the spelling bee came. As the contest went on, more and more students had to go back to their seats, having missed the words they were given. By the final round, as was expected by everyone, Patrick and Melissa were the only two students left standing in the competition.

9. Read this sentence from the passage.

He knew, though, that his best friend, Melissa Sanchez, would provide stiff competition.

Which of these is the best paraphrase of this sentence?

Ⓐ He knew that Melissa Sanchez had been in the competition before.

Ⓑ He knew that his friend Melissa Sanchez would be hard to beat.

Ⓒ He knew that after the contest, Melissa Sanchez would be his best friend.

Ⓓ He wanted to be best friends with Melissa Sanchez, but he knew that she was stiff.

Harcourt • Reading and Language Skills Assessment

COMPREHENSION: Paraphrase (continued)

10. Read this sentence from the passage.

By the final round, as was expected by everyone, Patrick and Melissa were the only two students left standing in the competition.

Which of these is the best paraphrase of this sentence?

Ⓐ At the end, just as everyone expected, Patrick and Melissa were the only two students still in the contest.

Ⓑ By the final round of the contest, even Patrick and Melissa were surprised.

Ⓒ Patrick and Melissa were the last two students anyone expected to be in a spelling competition.

Ⓓ I don't think anyone was surprised that Patrick and Melissa were students.

GO ON

COMPREHENSION: Paraphrase (continued)

Jared and his father were camping out within a short distance of a lake. They were sleeping in sleeping bags under a large tent. Very early one morning, Jared got up, picked up a spade and a tin can, went outside the tent, and began to dig up worms to use as bait. When he had all the worms the can could contain, he hurriedly reached for his fishing equipment.

"If we want to catch anything to cook for breakfast, we'd better get going, Jared," his dad said.

"I'm ready!" Jared answered. "I hope the fish are as hungry as I am!"

11. Read this sentence from the passage.

Jared and his father were camping out within a short distance of a lake.

Which of these is the best paraphrase of this sentence?

Ⓐ Jared's father wanted some distance between their camp and the lake.

Ⓑ Jared wanted to camp out with his father, but the distance to the lake was too short.

Ⓒ Jared and his dad were camping out near a lake.

Ⓓ Because of the lake a short distance away, Jared and his father wanted to camp out.

Lead the Way / Theme 6

Harcourt • Reading and Language Skills Assessment

COMPREHENSION: Paraphrase (continued)

12. Read this sentence from the passage.

When he had all the worms the can could contain, he hurriedly reached for his fishing equipment.

Which of these is the best paraphrase of this sentence?

Ⓐ When the can was full of worms, he grabbed his fishing pole.

Ⓑ He could not contain both the worms and his fishing equipment.

Ⓒ He was in a hurry to reach the fish, the worms, and the container.

Ⓓ He hoped the worms in the can would not reach his fishing equipment.

STOP

LANGUAGE

Directions: Read each question. Fill in the answer circle in front of the correct answer for each question.

13. Which is the correct contraction to replace the underlined words in this sentence?

    <u>I would</u> like to go, but I have to ask permission.
    (A) I'll
    (B) I'm
    (C) I've
    (D) I'd

14. Which is the correct contraction to replace the underlined words in this sentence?

    It is a good thing <u>we have</u> brought our umbrellas.
    (A) we've
    (B) we're
    (C) we'll
    (D) we'd

15. Which word is an adverb that tells *when* in this sentence?

    We often visit the city park to relax.
    (A) We
    (B) often
    (C) visit
    (D) park

LANGUAGE (continued)

16. Which word is an adverb that tells *how* in this sentence?

    She petted the kitten gently.

    (A) She

    (B) petted

    (C) kitten

    (D) gently

17. Which is the correct form of the adverb to complete this sentence?

    This jam spreads _____ than that jam.

    (A) more easily

    (B) most easily

    (C) more easier

    (D) most easiest

18. Which is the correct form of the adverb to complete this sentence?

    My kite is flying the_____ of all the kites.

    (A) more higher

    (B) most highest

    (C) highest

    (D) higher

19. Which word is a preposition in this sentence?

    Under the vast blue sky, we sat and talked.

    (A) Under

    (B) vast

    (C) we

    (D) sat

GO ON

LANGUAGE (continued)

20. Which word is the object of the preposition in this sentence?

For several months, my parents have been jogging daily.

Ⓐ several

Ⓑ months

Ⓒ parents

Ⓓ jogging

21. Which answer shows the prepositional phrase that tells *when* in this sentence?

After the rehearsal, the band members ate dinner and chatted.

Ⓐ After the rehearsal

Ⓑ the band members

Ⓒ ate dinner

Ⓓ and chatted

22. Which answer shows the prepositional phrase that tells *where* in this sentence?

The little girl carefully carried the tray to the table.

Ⓐ The little girl

Ⓑ carefully carried

Ⓒ the tray

Ⓓ to the table

Harcourt • Reading and Language Skills Assessment

· TROPHIES ·

New Lands / Theme 6
Reading and Language Skills Assessment

Harcourt

Orlando   Boston   Dallas   Chicago   San Diego

Part No. 9997-37752-4

ISBN 0-15-332203-9 (Package of 12)

4

• TROPHIES •

Reading and Language Skills
Assessment Posttest

Lead the Way / Theme 6

Name _____ Date _____

SKILL AREA	Criterion Score	Pupil Score	Pupil Strength
VOCABULARY Word Relationships	3/4	_____	_____
COMPREHENSION Fact and Opinion	3/4	_____	_____
Paraphrase	3/4	_____	_____
LANGUAGE Contractions and Negatives Adverbs Comparing with Adverbs Prepositions Prepositional Phrases	7/10	_____	_____
TOTAL SCORE	16/22	_____	_____

Were accommodations made in administering this test? ☐ Yes ☐ No

Type of accommodations: _____

_____

VOCABULARY: Word Relationships

Directions: Fill in the answer circle in front of the correct answer for each question.

1. Read this sentence.

   I have an opportunity to learn another language.

   Which word means about the **same** thing as *opportunity*?
   Ⓐ waste
   Ⓑ chance
   Ⓒ problem
   Ⓓ thought

2. Read this sentence.

   All this traveling has made me weary.

   Which word means the **opposite** of *weary*?
   Ⓐ cold
   Ⓑ unhappy
   Ⓒ scattered
   Ⓓ refreshed

3. How are the words *bare* and *bear* related?
   Ⓐ They are synonyms.
   Ⓑ They are antonyms.
   Ⓒ They are homophones.
   Ⓓ They are homographs.

4. How are the words *stop* and *halt* related?
   Ⓐ They are synonyms.
   Ⓑ They are antonyms.
   Ⓒ They are homophones.
   Ⓓ They are homographs.

STOP

COMPREHENSION: Fact and Opinion

Directions: Read the passage. Fill in the answer circle in front of the correct answer for each question.

At our school, we get only twenty-five minutes to eat lunch. This just isn't fair! It is impossible to eat in that amount of time. Many days I am only half finished eating when it's time to go outside for recess. If you had to cram your food down in such a short amount of time, you'd be upset, too! Just think about why we need more time. First, we are required to walk—not run—from our classroom to the cafeteria. Once we get there, we have to stand in line to get our food. After that, we have to stand in another line to pay for the food. There's got to be a faster way to get this done! Then we have to sit with our own class. That's another bad idea. Sometimes I want to sit with my friends in another class. Anyway, once we sit down and start eating, we have to gulp everything down fast or we won't get finished. There's a big stoplight in the cafeteria. When the light turns orange, we have only five minutes left. When the light turns red, lunch is over. Believe me, when I see the orange light, I really start chewing! This whole system needs to be changed. There is no good reason why we can't have more time for lunch. Someone should change this time immediately.

5. Which of these is a **fact** from the passage?
   Ⓐ This just isn't fair!
   Ⓑ You'd be upset, too!
   Ⓒ We get only twenty-five minutes for lunch.
   Ⓓ It is impossible to eat in that amount of time.

COMPREHENSION: Fact and Opinion (continued)

6. Which of these is an **opinion** from the passage?
   (A) We are required to walk—not run—from our classroom to the cafeteria.
   (B) We have to stand in line to get our food.
   (C) We have to stand in another line to pay for the food.
   (D) There's got to be a faster way to get this done!

7. Which of these is a **fact** from the passage?
   (A) That's another bad idea.
   (B) We have to sit with our own class.
   (C) This whole system needs to be changed.
   (D) There is no good reason why we can't have more time for lunch.

8. Which of these is an **opinion** from the passage?
   (A) Someone should change this time immediately.
   (B) There's a big stoplight in the cafeteria.
   (C) When the light turns orange, we have only five minutes left.
   (D) When the light turns red, lunch is over.

STOP

COMPREHENSION: Paraphrase

Directions: Read the passage. Fill in the answer circle in front of the correct answer for each question.

Kerry and his classmates are excited that their assignment will be doing research on the pyramids of Egypt. Each student will learn something different about the pyramids. After school, Kerry goes to the public library, finds the section that has sets of encyclopedia, and takes Volume *P* from the shelf. He opens the encyclopedia, buries his face in the book for some time, and copies down important ideas from the reading. Then he puts the book back on the shelf.

9. Read this sentence from the passage.

Kerry and his classmates are excited that their assignment will be doing research on the pyramids of Egypt.

Which of these is the best paraphrase of this sentence?

Ⓐ Kerry's class finds research and assignments exciting.

Ⓑ Kerry's class is excited about studying the Egyptian pyramids.

Ⓒ Kerry's class will be researching the pyramids of Egypt for an assignment.

Ⓓ Kerry's class is going to see the pyramids of Egypt at the end of the research assignment.

Harcourt • Reading and Language Skills Assessment

COMPREHENSION: Paraphrase (continued)

10. Read this sentence from the passage.

He opens the encyclopedia, buries his face in the book for some time, and copies down important ideas from the reading.

Which of these is the best paraphrase of this sentence?

(A) Since the encyclopedia is open, he copies all the ideas from it.

(B) He opens the encyclopedia to a page that tells about how to copy faces.

(C) He opens the encyclopedia, reads for a while, and takes notes about what he has read.

(D) He opens the encyclopedia so that he can hide his face behind the book for some time.

GO ON

COMPREHENSION: Paraphrase (continued)

Pete wasn't looking forward to spending two weeks with his grandparents in the city. He much preferred to stay at home and find pleasure in his friends' company. What was there to do in the city?

Pete's mom left him at his grandparents' place late one evening. He figured they'd tell him it was time for bed. Instead, Grandpa looked at Pete with a twinkle in his eye and asked, "Do you like music, Pete? There's a jazz festival going on, and Grandma and I are planning to go for a couple of hours. Does that sound good to you?" Pete was especially fond of jazz, so the idea held a great deal of appeal for him.

11. Read this sentence from the passage.

He much preferred to stay at home and find pleasure in his friends' company.

Which of these is the best paraphrase of this sentence?
Ⓐ He wanted to stay home and have a good time with his friends.
Ⓑ He and his friends liked staying at home more than having pleasure.
Ⓒ He preferred to work at his friends' company instead of staying home.
Ⓓ He preferred that his friends go instead of him.

12. Read this sentence from the passage.

Pete was especially fond of jazz, so the idea held a great deal of appeal for him.

Which of these is the best paraphrase of this sentence?
Ⓐ Pete liked jazz and making good deals.
Ⓑ Pete loved jazz, so that sounded great to him.
Ⓒ Pete was appealing, and he was fond of jazz.
Ⓓ Great jazz made people fond of Pete.

Harcourt • Reading and Language Skills Assessment

LANGUAGE

Directions: Read each question. Fill in the answer circle in front of the correct answer for each question.

13. Which is the correct contraction to replace the underlined words in this sentence?

    <u>You are</u> going to be late if you don't hurry.
    (A) You've
    (B) You're
    (C) You'll
    (D) You'd

14. Which is the correct contraction to replace the underlined words in this sentence?

    Pete and Sara said <u>they would</u> bring the picnic lunch.
    (A) they've
    (B) they're
    (C) they'd
    (D) they'll

15. Which word is an adverb that tells *how* in this sentence?

    She carefully picked each egg from the nest.
    (A) She
    (B) carefully
    (C) picked
    (D) nest

GO ON

LANGUAGE (continued)

16. Which word is an adverb that tells *when* in this sentence?

Finally, we are leaving on our vacation trip.

Ⓐ Finally

Ⓑ we

Ⓒ leaving

Ⓓ vacation

17. Which is the correct form of the adverb to complete this sentence?

I worked _____ than last time.

Ⓐ fastest

Ⓑ most fastest

Ⓒ faster

Ⓓ more faster

18. Which is the correct form of the adverb to complete this sentence?

He may not be the best athlete, but he tries the _____ of all.

Ⓐ more harder

Ⓑ most hardest

Ⓒ harder

Ⓓ hardest

19. Which word is a preposition in this sentence?

In the huge auditorium, the audience cheered and clapped.

Ⓐ In

Ⓑ huge

Ⓒ audience

Ⓓ cheered

Harcourt • Reading and Language Skills Assessment

GO ON

LANGUAGE (continued)

20. Which answer is the object of the preposition in this sentence?

The children at Roosevelt School have a new playground.

Ⓐ children
Ⓑ Roosevelt School
Ⓒ have
Ⓓ playground

21. Which answer shows the prepositional phrase that tells *when* in this sentence?

Before the game, the team members ran laps and did sit-ups.

Ⓐ Before the game
Ⓑ the team members
Ⓒ ran laps
Ⓓ did sit-ups

22. Which answer shows the prepositional phrase that tells *where* in this sentence?

The brown leather jacket on the chair is mine.

Ⓐ The brown
Ⓑ leather jacket
Ⓒ on the chair
Ⓓ is mine

STOP

New Lands / Theme 6

Reading and Language Skills Assessment

Harcourt

Orlando   Boston   Dallas   Chicago   San Diego

Part No. 9997-37746-X

ISBN 0-15-332203-9 (Package of 12)

4

TROPHIES

End-of-Year Reading and Language Skills Assessment

Lead the Way/Themes 1-6

Name _____ Date _____

SKILL AREA	Criterion Score	Pupil Score	Pupil Strength
VOCABULARY	4/6	_____	_____
COMPREHENSION	18/24	_____	_____
RESEARCH AND INFORMATION SKILLS	3/4	_____	_____
LANGUAGE	12/16	_____	_____
TOTAL SCORE	**37/50**	_____	_____

Were accommodations made in administering this test? ☐ Yes ☐ No

Type of accommodations: _____

_____

VOCABULARY

Directions: Fill in the answer circle in front of the correct answer for each question.

1. I'm sorry, but I can't respray your yard.

What does the word *respray* mean?
Ⓐ spray before
Ⓑ spray again
Ⓒ bad spray
Ⓓ spray between

2. Which suffix can be added to the word *fear* to make it mean "without fear"?
Ⓐ able
Ⓑ er
Ⓒ less
Ⓓ ful

3. Read this sentence.

Did you locate your lost jacket?

Which word means about the **same** thing as *locate*?
Ⓐ find
Ⓑ change
Ⓒ empty
Ⓓ lighten

VOCABULARY (continued)

4. Read this sentence.

   What time did Juan arrive?

   Which word means the **opposite** of *arrive*?
   Ⓐ say
   Ⓑ fall
   Ⓒ appear
   Ⓓ leave

5. How are the words *rain* and *rein* related?
   Ⓐ They are synonyms.
   Ⓑ They are antonyms.
   Ⓒ They are homophones.
   Ⓓ They are homographs.

6. How are the words *true* and *false* related?
   Ⓐ They are synonyms.
   Ⓑ They are antonyms.
   Ⓒ They are homophones.
   Ⓓ They are homographs.

Harcourt • Reading and Language Skills Assessment

COMPREHENSION

Directions: Read each passage. Then read the questions that follow the passage. Fill in the answer circle in front of the correct answer for each question.

Beatrix Potter
Her Characters and Books

The name *Beatrix Potter* may not be familiar to you. However, you might know some of the characters Potter created, such as Peter Rabbit, Jemima Puddleduck, and Mrs. Tiggy-Winkle. Beatrix Potter was a British author and illustrator. She is known for writing such popular children's books as *The Tale of Peter Rabbit*, *The Tale of Squirrel Nutkin*, and *The Tale of Benjamin Bunny*. *The Tale of Peter Rabbit* is probably the best children's book ever written.

How She Became a Writer

When Beatrix was a child, her family took her on holidays to Scotland and to the English Lake District. These beautiful locations aroused in Beatrix a love of animals and of the countryside. After she grew up and was in her twenties, she still went on holidays to Scotland. In 1893 during one of these holidays, she wrote a letter to a sick child. She told the child, Noel, a story about four rabbits named Flopsy, Mopsy, Peter, and Cottontail. She drew pictures to go along with the story. The story turned out so well that she decided to have it published. It was such a success that she went on to write more than twenty other children's books. She designed the books to be quite small so that even tiny children could hold them to read, and she did all the watercolor pictures herself. Beatrix Potter's books are still loved by children all over the world.

Harcourt • Reading and Language Skills Assessment

GO ON

COMPREHENSION (continued)

7. The section **Her Characters and Books** is mainly organized by _____.

Ⓐ main idea and details

Ⓑ comparison and contrast

Ⓒ cause and effect

Ⓓ sequence of events

8. Which of these is an **opinion** from the passage?

Ⓐ When Beatrix was a child, Beatrix's family took her on holidays to Scotland.

Ⓑ Beatrix Potter was a British author and illustrator.

Ⓒ *The Tale of Peter Rabbit* is probably the best children's book ever written.

Ⓓ Beatrix Potter went on to write more than twenty other children's books.

9. Read this sentence from the passage.

These beautiful locations aroused in Beatrix a love of animals and of the countryside.

Which statement is the best paraphrase of this sentence?

Ⓐ The animals in the countryside loved Beatrix because she was beautiful.

Ⓑ These pretty places inspired Beatrix's love of animals and the countryside.

Ⓒ These locations were beautiful to Beatrix and to the animals in the countryside.

Ⓓ The animals in the countryside aroused in Beatrix a love of beautiful locations.

COMPREHENSION (continued)

10. According to this passage, who was Noel?
   Ⓐ a character in one of Beatrix Potter's books
   Ⓑ Beatrix Potter's pet rabbit
   Ⓒ the name of Beatrix Potter's first publisher
   Ⓓ a sick child for whom Beatrix Potter wrote a story

11. Which of these happened **first** in the passage?
   Ⓐ In 1893 Beatrix Potter wrote a story about four rabbits.
   Ⓑ Beatrix Potter decided to have her story about four rabbits published.
   Ⓒ Beatrix Potter's family took her on holidays when she was a child.
   Ⓓ Beatrix Potter wrote twenty more children's books.

12. Why did Beatrix Potter design her books to be very small?
   Ⓐ to save on the cost of paper
   Ⓑ so that children could hold them
   Ⓒ because the stories were very short
   Ⓓ because the animals in the books were little

COMPREHENSION (continued)

Armor is a type of covering used to protect the body. Throughout history, people have used armor for protection during combat. As long ago as the Stone Age, people wore layers of animal skins to protect them from blows from clubs or axes. Everyone knows that animal skins don't offer much protection, though. Later, people carried metal shields to protect them during fighting. In time, armor became a covering for the whole body. During the Middle Ages, a knight wore a suit of heavy armor that covered him from head to toe. He wore a leather tunic under his armor. To protect his head, he wore a helmet with a face covering called a *visor*. He even wore armored gloves, called *gauntlets*, to protect his hands. Sometimes the horse a knight rode had armor on its head and body for protection as well. It probably wasn't smart to wear so much armor, because it would weigh a knight down too much to move easily. The *armorers* who made the knights' armor started decorating the outside of the armor with silver, gold, and precious jewels. It seems like a silly idea to try to look fancy when going into battle, but that's what they did. Armor eventually got so strong that it couldn't be pierced with a lance. A knight would just try to knock his opponent off his horse when he couldn't pierce the armor.

Harcourt • Reading and Language Skills Assessment

COMPREHENSION (continued)

13. What is the main idea of this passage?

Ⓐ Later, people carried metal shields to protect them during fighting.

Ⓑ Throughout history, people have used armor for protection during combat.

Ⓒ As long ago as the Stone Age, people wore layers of animal skins to protect them.

Ⓓ A knight wore a suit of heavy armor that covered him from head to toe.

14. Which of these is a **fact** from the passage?

Ⓐ Everyone knows that animal skins don't offer much protection.

Ⓑ It probably wasn't smart to wear so much armor.

Ⓒ Sometimes the horse a knight rode had armor on its head and body.

Ⓓ It seems like a silly idea to try to look fancy when going into battle.

15. What was the author's purpose in writing this passage?

Ⓐ to inform

Ⓑ to persuade

Ⓒ to warn

Ⓓ to entertain

GO ON

COMPREHENSION (continued)

16. What are the armored gloves a knight wore to protect his hands called?

Ⓐ armorers

Ⓑ visors

Ⓒ shields

Ⓓ gauntlets

17. The face covering of a knight's helmet is called a _____.

Ⓐ lance

Ⓑ armorer

Ⓒ visor

Ⓓ tunic

COMPREHENSION (continued)

"Good afternoon, boys and girls, and welcome to our show. I've got a joke for you. What's black and white and read all over?" Nathan asked members of the audience. Nathan and two of his friends, Rosa and George, were putting on a talent show in Nathan's garage. They had charged their friends twenty-five cents to see the show. Now they were struggling to keep the audience entertained. The crowd was beginning to get restless. There were whispers and rumblings of discontent.

"A newspaper! A newspaper is black and white and read all over. Yuk, yuk, yuk!" Nathan finished his joke, trying to milk a laugh out of the crowd. Instead, he heard a low groan. Nathan knew it was time to try another act. "And now, boys and girls, I give you George, the amazing juggler!"

At that point, George walked out, juggling three red balls that he'd been practicing with all week. To everyone's surprise—even George's— the juggling went pretty well. Things were picking up. After George's act, Nathan announced Rosa. She came out carrying a red-white-and- blue flag and wearing red slacks, a white blouse, and a blue hair ribbon. She began to sing "I'm a Yankee Doodle Dandy." After a ner- vous start, her voice began to get stronger. She even started to enjoy all the attention. She added a few dance steps to the singing and tried to sound like the professional singers she'd heard on television. When she finished, everyone clapped and cheered.

"Great show, guys," a guest said after the show was over. "The next time you present a performance, you could even raise the price of admission to fifty cents!"

GO ON

COMPREHENSION (continued)

18. What is the best summary of this passage?

Ⓐ Nathan finished a joke and tried to milk a laugh out of the audience.

Ⓑ Nathan, Rosa, and George told jokes, juggled, and sang to entertain the audience at a talent show in Nathan's garage.

Ⓒ There were whispers and rumblings of discontent in the audience at a talent show in Nathan's garage.

Ⓓ Rosa carried a flag and tried to sound like the professional singers she'd heard on television.

19. Read this sentence from the passage.

"The next time you present a performance, you could even raise the price of admission to fifty cents!"

Which is the best paraphrase of this statement?

Ⓐ We will pay you fifty cents not to put on another performance.

Ⓑ The next time you put on a show, you could charge fifty cents to get in.

Ⓒ The next time you put on a performance, you might make fifty cents.

Ⓓ At your next performance, you should give presents that cost fifty cents.

20. Which of these happened **last** in the passage?

Ⓐ Rosa sang and danced.

Ⓑ George juggled three red balls.

Ⓒ Nathan told the audience a joke.

Ⓓ Nathan welcomed boys and girls to the show.

21. Why did the author write this passage?

Ⓐ to persuade readers to be in a talent show

Ⓑ to inform readers about ways to become more talented

Ⓒ to entertain readers with a story about a talent show

Ⓓ to warn readers not to attend a talent show

GO ON

Harcourt • Reading and Language Skills Assessment

COMPREHENSION (continued)

Jumping Mice

Description of Jumping Mice

A *jumping mouse* is a small rodent that hops around on its hind legs. Jumping mice are very interesting animals. They have long back legs and extremely long tails. An average jumping mouse's body is about four inches long, but its tail is about five inches long. Jumping mice look really funny with tails longer than their bodies.

Where Jumping Mice Live

Jumping mice can be found in North America, Europe, and Asia. In North America, they usually live in meadows and in shrubs or small trees along the edge of woods. They seem to prefer damp places.

Food, Winter Sleep, and Babies

Jumping mice eat berries, leaves and stems, and insects. They are different from most other mice because they *hibernate*, or sleep through the winter. One female jumping mouse can give birth to two litters in a year. She usually has about five baby mice in each litter.

22. The section **Description of Jumping Mice** is mainly organized by _____.

   Ⓐ main idea and details

   Ⓑ comparison and contrast

   Ⓒ cause and effect

   Ⓓ sequence of events

GO ON

COMPREHENSION (continued)

23. What is the main idea of this passage?

Ⓐ Jumping mice have long back legs and long tails.

Ⓑ Jumping mice are very interesting animals.

Ⓒ Jumping mice usually live in meadows, shrubs, or small trees.

Ⓓ Jumping mice can be found in North America, Europe, and Asia.

24. Which of these is an **opinion** from the passage?

Ⓐ Jumping mice *hibernate*, or sleep through the winter.

Ⓑ Jumping mice eat berries, leaves and stems, and insects.

Ⓒ An average jumping mouse's body is about four inches long.

Ⓓ Jumping mice look really funny with tails longer than their bodies.

25. How many baby mice does a female jumping mouse usually have in a year?

Ⓐ one

Ⓑ ten

Ⓒ twenty

Ⓓ thirty

26. Why did the author write this passage?

Ⓐ to inform readers about the jumping mouse

Ⓑ to persuade readers to get a pet jumping mouse

Ⓒ to warn readers not to touch or feed a jumping mouse

Ⓓ to entertain readers with funny stories about a jumping mouse

Harcourt • Reading and Language Skills Assessment

COMPREHENSION (continued)

Directions: Read the passage. Fill in the answer circle in front of the correct answer for each question.

Karen's mother showed her how to send a fax to someone. A fax machine is like a telephone that sends pages of writing instead of spoken words. Here are the steps Karen's mother wrote down:

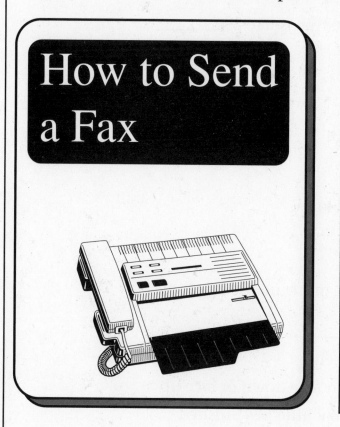

1. Place the paper you want to send face down in the fax machine.
2. Dial the number of the fax machine you are calling (just like when using a telephone).
3. Press the button marked "Start."
4. The fax machine will send a copy of your paper to the machine you called.
5. When the fax machine has finished, remember to remove your paper.

GO ON

COMPREHENSION (continued)

27. What should Karen do **first** to send the fax?
    - Ⓐ Press the button marked "Start."
    - Ⓑ Dial the number of the fax machine she is calling.
    - Ⓒ Place the paper she wants to send face down in the machine.
    - Ⓓ Remove the paper.

28. The passage says that a fax machine is like a _____.
    - Ⓐ car
    - Ⓑ radio
    - Ⓒ television
    - Ⓓ telephone

29. What should Karen do **last**?
    - Ⓐ Press the button marked "Start."
    - Ⓑ Remove the paper.
    - Ⓒ Hang up the receiver.
    - Ⓓ Dial the number of the fax machine she is calling.

30. The passage does **not** tell _____.
    - Ⓐ how many pages you can send
    - Ⓑ whether to put the paper in face down or face up
    - Ⓒ what to do when the fax machine has finished
    - Ⓓ which button to press to send a fax

STOP

Score _____

Lead the Way / End-of-Year Skills

Harcourt • Reading and Language Skills Assessment

RESEARCH AND INFORMATION SKILLS

Directions: Fill in the answer circle in front of the **best** answer for each question.

31. Where would you look to find a synonym for the word *avoid*?
- (A) thesaurus
- (B) encyclopedia
- (C) almanac
- (D) atlas

32. What would be the **best** source for information for a report on dolphins?
- (A) atlas
- (B) dictionary
- (C) encyclopedia
- (D) newspaper

33. Where would you look to find out the names of the people serving on the United States Supreme Court?
- (A) atlas
- (B) almanac
- (C) dictionary
- (D) thesaurus

34. Where would you look to find out which states the Mississippi River runs through?
- (A) atlas
- (B) dictionary
- (C) thesaurus
- (D) telephone directory

STOP

LANGUAGE

Directions: Read each question. Fill in the answer circle in front of the correct answer for each question.

35. Which group of words is a sentence?
    - Ⓐ Had fresh flowers and boxes of candy.
    - Ⓑ Overlooking the wide green valley.
    - Ⓒ All the guests have keys to their rooms.
    - Ⓓ The small, frisky puppy with a brown collar.

36. Which answer best describes this group of words?

    Today we planted some laurel trees, and next week we will plant roses.
    - Ⓐ simple sentence
    - Ⓑ compound sentence
    - Ⓒ complex sentence
    - Ⓓ dependent clause

37. Which word is an object pronoun in this sentence?

    Toby said that he would bring the lessons to me.
    - Ⓐ Toby
    - Ⓑ said
    - Ⓒ would
    - Ⓓ me

38. Which pronoun correctly completes this sentence?

    My sister said I could have all the stickers that are _____.
    - Ⓐ my
    - Ⓑ your
    - Ⓒ hers
    - Ⓓ our

Harcourt • Reading and Language Skills Assessment

LANGUAGE (continued)

39. Which word is an adjective in this sentence?

Many children won prizes at the fair.

Ⓐ Many

Ⓑ children

Ⓒ won

Ⓓ fair

40. Which adjective correctly completes this sentence?

My brother is _____ than my father.

Ⓐ more taller

Ⓑ most tallest

Ⓒ taller

Ⓓ tallest

41. Which word is the action verb in this sentence?

The shuttle roared into space.

Ⓐ shuttle

Ⓑ roared

Ⓒ into

Ⓓ space

42. Which word is the helping verb in this sentence?

We have seen this movie before.

Ⓐ We

Ⓑ have

Ⓒ seen

Ⓓ movie

GO ON

LANGUAGE (continued)

43. Which word is the linking verb in this sentence?

The gentleman in the gray suit is my neighbor.

Ⓐ gentleman

Ⓑ gray

Ⓒ suit

Ⓓ is

44. Which present-tense verb agrees with the subject in this sentence?

A recent report says that dolphins _____ themselves in a mirror.

Ⓐ recognize

Ⓑ recognizes

Ⓒ recognized

Ⓓ will recognize

45. Which is the correct past-tense verb to complete this sentence?

Yesterday we _____ a film about volcanoes.

Ⓐ watch

Ⓑ watches

Ⓒ watched

Ⓓ will watch

46. Which is the correct future-tense verb to complete this sentence?

Soon we _____ what the big surprise is!

Ⓐ know

Ⓑ knows

Ⓒ knew

Ⓓ will know

GO ON

Lead the Way / End-of-Year Skills

LANGUAGE (continued)

47. Which is the correct contraction to replace the underlined words in this sentence?

After we eat, <u>we will</u> go to a movie.

Ⓐ we've

Ⓑ we'll

Ⓒ we've

Ⓓ we'd

48. Which word is an adverb that tells *how* in this sentence?

We listened carefully to the story.

Ⓐ We

Ⓑ listened

Ⓒ carefully

Ⓓ story

49. Which is the correct form of the adverb to complete this sentence?

That man is running _____ than the other man.

Ⓐ fastest

Ⓑ faster

Ⓒ more faster

Ⓓ most fastest

50. Which answer shows the prepositional phrase that tells *when* in this sentence?

Before dinner, my brother and sister made a salad and set the table.

Ⓐ Before dinner

Ⓑ my brother and sister

Ⓒ made a salad

Ⓓ set the table

STOP

· T R O P H I E S ·

Lead the Way / Themes 1-6
End-of-Year Reading and Language Skills Assessment

Harcourt

Orlando   Boston   Dallas   Chicago   San Diego

Part No. 9997-37754-0

ISBN 0-15-332203-9 (Package of 12)